ROBIN LAING is one of those lucky indi  d
interests into a career. On the one h; ;
Scotland's most important export, her mc _
haps her greatest contribution to humani e
Scotch Malt Whisky Society and writes ma. _
tions. He also contributes regularly to *Whisky Magazine* and has published *The Whisky Muse*, a collection of poems and songs on the subject of Scotch whisky, and *The Whisky River: The Distilleries of Speyside* (both Luath Press).

On the other hand, Robin is also a musician. As a songwriter and interpreter of traditional Scots song, he has recorded seven CDs. Three of those are whisky CDs; *The Angels' Share* (1997), *The Water of Life* (2003) and *One for the Road* (2007).

Robin performs his 'Whisky and Song' shows all over the world, thus being an ambassador for Scotland in the most enjoyable way imaginable.

Robin was born in Edinburgh in 1953 and now lives in rural South Lanarkshire. He loves beach barbeques, star-gazing and walking in the mountains.

BOB DEWAR was born in Edinburgh at an early age. Sixteen years later he was published nationally. He worked in DC Thomson's studio where, among other things, he ghosted Dennis the Menace. After going freelance, he did political and social commentary for *The Scotsman* newspaper. He has illustrated books for many publishers including the Children's and English Speaking Departments of Oxford University Press, and for Fife Educational Social Development. His work has also appeared in *The Times, The Herald, Scottish Field* and The Scotch Malt Whisky Society newsletter and on its Members Room ceiling. He has had exhibitions in Lucca, Italy, in Glasgow and in Edinburgh and had caricatures hanging in the House of Commons. He is now a lot older than 16 and is married to the novelist Isla Dewar, with two sons and an absurdly friendly big golden retriever. Bob has no idea how this friendliness happened, since he tends toward grumpiness.

Whisky Legends of Islay

ROBIN LAING

Luath Press Limited

EDINBURGH

www.luath.co.uk

First published 2009
Reprinted 2010

ISBN: 978-1-906817-11-4

The paper used in this book is recyclable. It is made from low chlorine pulps produced in a low energy, low emissions manner from renewable forests.

Printed and bound by Bell & Bain Ltd., Glasgow

Typeset in 10.5 point Mrs Eaves by 3btype.com

Map by Jim Lewis

Illustrations by Bob Dewar

ACKNOWLEDGEMENTS

I am particularly indebted to Bowmore distillery, who set me off on the track of Islay's legends, and to Bruichladdich, who keep me on it. I also drew inspiration from Andrew Jefford's book, *Peat Smoke and Spirit*.

In addition I would like to thank the following individuals and organisations;

John Baker, James Brown, The Michael Bruce Memorial Trust, Jenni Calder, David Campbell, John Campbell (Laphroaig), Kevin Campbell (Lagavulin), Trevor Cowan, Richard Drew, Famedram Publishers, David Gibb, Eric J. Graham, John Grant (Glenfarclas), Janette Hannah, Harold Hastie, Michael Heads (Ardbeg), Lennart Hellsing, Iain Henderson, Bruno Hofweber (Rugenbräu Brewery), The Lanarkshire Songwriters, Christine Logan, Graham Logie (Lagavulin), Eddie MacAffer (Bowmore), Andy Macdonald (Ionad Chaluim Chille Ile), Jim and Barbara McEwan (Bruichladdich), Duncan McGillivray (Bruichladdich), Jamie MacKenzie (Bowmore), John MacLellan (Bunnahabhain), Iseabail MacTaggart (Bowmore), John Malcolm, Wallace Milroy, Gordon Neil, Martine Nouet, Hans Offringa, Malcolm Ogilvie (Port Charlotte Museum), Jim Porter (Fleetwood Trawlers), Carl Reavey (*The Ileach*), Mark and Maureen Reynier (Bruichladdich), Edith Ryan, Neil Scott (Harbour Inn, Bowmore), The Scottish Poetry Library, Billy Stewart, Billy Stitchell (Caol Ila), Jackie Thompson (Ardbeg), Hamish Torrie (Ardbeg), Anthony Wills (Kilchoman).

CONTENTS

ISLANDS

Song by Robin Laing – recorded on *Ebb and Flow* (Whistleberry CD001)

There's an island in the sea
I can feel it calling me
It's sometimes far, sometimes near
Sometimes the weather makes it disappear

The tide runs in, the tide runs out
In a way that's what life's about
Day and night, to and fro
The cycle of the seasons the ebb and flow

CHORUS
As long as we can think beyond horizons
We will be drawn to islands
Not sure of what we might find
But as we come and as we go
The one thing we can't know
Is what we will leave behind.

Island people understand
Close to the sea means close to the land
Out of mid-stream, a place apart
Message in a bottle on the swell of the heart

We are sailors in the night
Guided by a flashing light
The sea runs deep, the sea runs fast
Ulysses kisses the shore at last

CHORUS
As long as we can think beyond horizons
We will be drawn to islands
Not sure of what we might find
But as we come and as we go
The one thing we can't know
Is what we will leave behind.

We leave walls and standing stones
We leave stories and weathered bones
We leave a trail a mile wide
Washed away by the following tide.
However much we touch the land
We are driftwood on the sand.

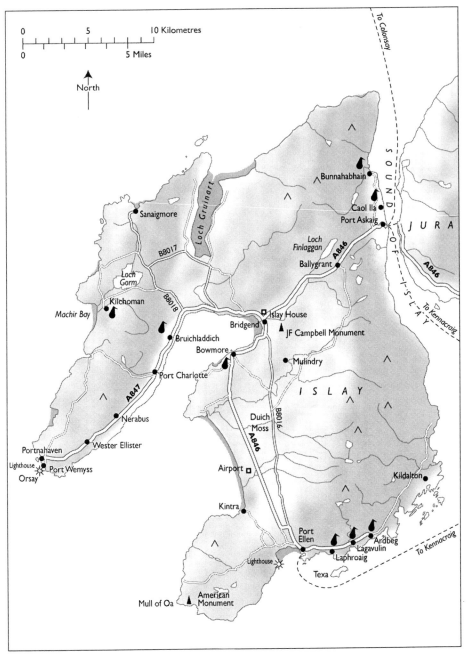

INTRODUCTION

There is something special about Islay. Some would say (I am one of them) that every island has something special to offer, and Scotland is indeed lucky to be blessed with so many islands of beauty and character. Yet even among this jewel box of island gems, Islay is known as the Queen of the Hebrides.

For many people, the thing that makes Islay so special is her whisky. Fair enough; she certainly has more distilleries than other islands, indeed more than all the other islands put together. The flow of whisky running from Islay, per capita, may well be the most impressive anywhere in the world. If the tax revenue generated by Islay was all given back, her population would be the richest in Britain.

Quantity is easy to measure; quality, on the other hand, is essentially a subjective matter. However, it can also be measured in some ways, and in terms of sales, awards and scores given by respected whisky writers, Islay malts do very well indeed; they are all high quality whiskies.

Not all Islay malts are smoky beasts by any means but the majority of her distilleries do produce malts that are invigorated to some degree by peat-smoke. Some people, having discovered peaty whiskies, find it hard to go back, just as many people find it impossible to go back to blends once they have graduated to the world of single malts. Personally, I love the diversity of single malts and Islay certainly has that. Of course there are some who shun smoky whiskies, but there are others who proudly assert that they drink nothing else – to me either position is a bit like refusing to date blondes or like trying to paint the blues out of a rainbow.

Yes, Islay is the whisky island, and her whisky history is fascinating: how production moved from small, private stills to farm distilling and then to much larger units; how Islay whiskies did well when the sea was the main highway of trade and how most of them have survived into a new age when transport presents different challenges; how distilling became so concentrated on Islay, perhaps as a result of the lack of an Excise presence for 90 years, The story of the lost distilleries of Islay is fascinating, and so is the modern phenomenon of how whisky draws tourists and visitors to the island in large numbers, contributing to the economy in additional ways.

However, Islay has much more than whisky. She has a wonderful landscape, as diverse as the whiskies that come from it; from miles of aromatic, squelchy peat bog to miles of beautiful sandy beaches (sometimes also aromatic and squelchy but usually ozone-fresh and Mediterranean), from bleak, remote mountains to sheltered woodland and from secret rivers and lochs to the long sea-indented coastline of rocky shores, pebble beaches and towering cliffs.

Islay has wildlife too – fishing and bird-watching attract many visitors to the island. Red deer, hares and mountain goats all give Islay a wild, close-to-nature feel, which somehow complements the island's important farming enterprises.

Islay has a captivating history. Waves of people have come here over centuries leaving their mark — the first hunter-gatherers, the Iron Age farmers and settlers, the Viking raiders who came back to settle this fertile island and the holy men, spreading Christianity, many of them from nearby Ireland. Islay has always attracted people; it is no surprise that the seafaring Lords of the Isles chose Islay as the heart of their empire.

All these different peoples coming to put roots down on Islay, the tendency Ileachs have to travel (missionaries, drovers, Lords of the Isles, whisky ambassadors) and the interface between Nordic, Gaelic and English-speaking worlds have all given Islay a rich culture. Perhaps even more than other parts of Scotland, Islay is a land of story-tellers. History and folklore have combined to produce a people who love to tell stories and through the telling and re-telling of stories, legends are born.

Being a whisky island, it is not surprising that many of these legends have a whisky element. The story cupboard of Islay is very full indeed and whisky tales are only one shelf, but I have chosen to concentrate on that shelf because whisky is my passion. The reader will discover that some of the stories have whisky connections that are slightly tenuous or even contrived. I make no apology for that; whisky is a thread whose distinct colour runs through the fabric of these tales, indeed it is the thread that holds them together but it cannot be the only thread that story cloths are made of.

I present here a patchwork of tales; there are historical stories and Celtic legends drawn from the oral tradition but often found in books and the internet; there are also accounts of more recent events, based on things I have been told, things I have uncovered and one or two creations of my own imagination — it is after all a book of legends.

My experience of Islay is not as extensive as I would like it to have been. I have travelled there on numerous occasions, through my whisky work, or simply for pleasure and holidays. I have no family connections with the place and I have never lived there. I do feel, however, that I have a spiritual connection. Whenever I travel to Islay I feel happy with the excitement of anticipation and whenever it is time to leave I feel sad. Whenever I am there I have adventures.

I hope this book conveys some of the pleasure I have gained from visiting Islay and some of my regard for that beautiful, fascinating island and her people, whom I have always found to be warm, straightforward, entertaining and hospitable. From Islay I have learned that whisky is best taken with friends; but if friends are not available, stories will do.

SECTION ONE

THE POWER OF WHISKY

BAR LEGENDS

I have not been in every bar on Islay, though I have visited most of them. My friend Oliver Mühlmann, from Germany, did a complete Islay pub crawl once, with a couple of others (whose constitutions were hopefully as robust as that of the legendary Olli). They had a drink in every one in the course of a single day. Each bar has something interesting or quirky about it – I give only a taste here – further research is clearly needed.

An Tigh Seinnse

Every once in a while you come across a bar that seems, in a good way, to belong to a different age. An Tigh Seinnse, in Portnahaven, is such a place. It has character, quirkiness and a definite time-warp quality. The way it resembles someone's front parlour, the poky size, the fact that it has two separate and quite different rooms, the way you have to look up to the person serving behind the raised bar, the real fire, which is nearly always lit, all lend something of interest to one's first visit.

An Tigh Seinnse means House of Change or changehouse. It was once a coaching inn and the name would have referred to changing horses. Nowadays the locals joke that House of Change refers to the fact that you go in sober and come out drunk. But then, there could be something more fanciful, faery and camsteerie going on – maybe it's the kind of place where you can experience life-changing moments or encounters; the stuff of balladry and legend. Perhaps this is the obvious place where seal-folk would come to hang up their skins and enjoy a wee dram before sliding back into the ocean on winter nights.

Change houses feature in many of John Francis Campbell's tales; *The Handsome Lazy Lass, Alisdair, Son of the Emperor* and *The Two Skippers* all involve a change house and of course whisky. The tale of *Billy* also mentions a change house. Billy is an archetypal trickster who boasts that he can steal anything. In one part of the tale he manages to steal a horse by lying down among the pigs and pretending to be dead, with four bottles of whisky in his coat pockets, thus outwitting the horse's guards, who of course get drunk on the free whisky.

An Tigh Seinnse would have been the location, over generations, for the telling of such tales. Years ago it was run by a tremendous local character and entrepreneur called Charlie McKinnon. For years, Charlie ran both the hotel and his croft, multi-tasking in typical island style. During the war, the hotel did well; after the war he specialised in egg production and it became a kind of hen hotel.

In those days life had a quieter, steadier pace than now and routines could easily become established into traditions. One of those was the Friday night 'parliament' when all the men of the village came in to the bar after finishing work and were served a drink. Charlie then went off to milk the cows and no one could have a second drink until he returned. I could imagine conversation would continue to flow whether glasses were full or empty and the wrongs of the world might be put to rights.

Eventually Charlie became ill and died and his daughter Maureen took over the running of An Tigh Seinnse. She was thought by some to be a reluctant proprietor and had a bit of a reputation for being dour and difficult. She opened and closed the bar when it suited her and if she decided not to serve you, for whatever reason, then your 'bum was oot the windae', as they say in certain parts of Scotland.

I had heard of her reputation, but first met her when I fell into the bar early one evening with a group of musician friends. We had come to Islay on a song-writing project at the invitation of Jim McEwan, Bruichladdich's Production Director, and were also doing a concert in Portnahaven Hall. We ordered beers and fish teas, which were cooked and served by Maureen. She was polite and pleasant and the food was excellent. She must have over-heard some of our conversation and when the time came to pay the bill, she would not accept any money, saying with a chuckle, 'Tell Jim McEwan that's another favour he owes me!' I tell this story to counter the myth of grumpy Maureen and to give an example of the kind of hospitality frequently encountered on Islay.

In 2004, Maureen retired and Carl and Jan Reavey took over An Tigh Seinnse. It is now managed by the ever-friendly Janey Hanlon. I still go there whenever I can. It's the kind of place where you meet characters and in the tiny bar it is hard to avoid getting involved in conversation. The

spirit of the 'parliament' lives on. Surely this is what pubs should be about.

In front of An Tigh Seinnse, the ebb and flow of the tide turns Portnahaven cove into a screensaver on life. Seabirds and children forage the shore; seals slide on and off the rocks as the interplay between sea and sun dictates. Fishing boats come and go or just bob at their moorings. At night, the lighthouse birls out its eerie flashes of light while the sea is restless and seldom quiet. Here, at the farthest terminus of the long road from either of Islay's ferry ports, you sometimes feel that you have come to the edge of the world, only to feel its true pulse, and that your pilgrimage is complete.

The Wall of Coins

The Harbour Inn in Bowmore has a tiny public bar, which seems to expand Tardis-like, as more cheerful customers breeze through the door. A tradition has arisen whereby customers leave coins perched on ledges and in cracks all over the natural stone wall. The origins of this quaint custom are lost in the mist of time, so it only remains to speculate about the reason why it developed.

Is it a Trevi Fountain phenomenon, whereby visitors to the island deposit coins to ensure that fate will bring them here again?

Or, maybe someone from Seattle came here during the war and tried to recreate the Seattle gum wall, where people fix coins to a wall using chewing gum. In Seattle, spoil-sports frequently harvest the coins leaving only gum on the wall. In Bowmore in the 1940s maybe the locals harvested the gum and left the coins.

Or, perhaps after the notorious attack on the harbour in 1813 by the American privateer, the *True Blooded Yankee* (see page 69) a wave of patriotism and support for the British monarchy resulted in the publican at that time posting coins all over the wall, with the king's head facing the room.

Or, could it be that some local fishermen started it as a cushion against days when the weather, and therefore the catch was poor so that even if they had no cash they could glean sufficient coins from the wall to afford a wee dram.

Or, more prosaically, a rain-soaked tourist with a pocketful of change, and nothing better to do, spread coins around the wall out of boredom one day and the habit became established.

Then again, it reminds me of weird social phenomena like the Shoe Tree in America or the Bra Fence in New Zealand. Come to think of it, pinning bras to the wall in the Harbour Inn might possibly gain even more support.

There are various references (e.g. C. Gordon Booth, *An Islay Notebook*) to a local custom of putting coins in cracks in the stone at St Michael's Well, which is near Solam, north of Ardbeg. It appears this was a practice considered to bring good luck, especially to newlyweds. Sometimes horse shoes would also be placed near the well. This might hint at another explanation – drinkers, about to head for home, would place a coin on the wall of the pub, in the hope of getting an auspicious welcome from the wife when they finally arrived home.

The Islay Bar

The iconic Islay Bar was, in the old days, a most welcoming sight to travellers staggering off the ferry at Port Ellen after a rough crossing. Usually people stagger coming OUT of a pub – but not the Islay Bar! Then the hotel closed and for years it fell into decay, finally being demolished in 2008. Soon a new establishment will rise from the ashes, but will it be a revitalized Islay Bar? It would be sad to see a much-copied icon disappear completely.

There is an Islay Bar in Tokyo (where you can 'enjoy Rippongi night life'), and one in Okinawa, that specializes in couscous. The Islay Inn in Glasgow, is home to the Glasgow Fiddle Club, and there is one in Munich.

The Islay Bar in Munich is run by Ulrike Putz who, on the website, tells how the inspiration to open a bar named after her favourite island and style of whisky came in a dream. She was in a pub in Edinburgh with such legendary whisky people as Michael Jackson, Murray McDavid (sic), the Heart Brothers (sic), the Signatory brothers (sic) and Her Majesty the Queen (who was drinking Guinness – perhaps also sic). Michael told Ulrike it was her destiny to open a good whisky bar in Munich and the Queen offered to work as the barmaid. The rest is history.

POSTSCRIPT: it appears that just as the last part of the original Islay Bar was being bulldozed in late 2008, the Islay Bar in Munich also closed. The rumour is that Ulrike Putz is planning to re-open in new premises; good luck Ulrike, with your quest to find new premises and to replace Lizzie, the popular barmaid.

ISLAY CHEESE

The poem that follows is from *The Compleat Angus: The Life and Works of Angus Macintyre of Taynuilt and Tobermory* (Famedram Publishers, 1989). Angus Macintyre was not the only one to be inspired by the legend of Islay cheese and its famed aphrodisiacal qualities; a musical play *Hard Pressed* was written by Dave Smith a few years ago and performed in the Edinburgh Festival Fringe to some acclaim.

ISLAY CHEESE

(Whose import into Italy was banned several years ago because of its alleged aphrodisiac qualities.)

You Highland women I implore
Upon my bended knees,
Please do not eat one morsel more
Of that awful Islay Cheese.

No more the 'Tallies' smack their lips
O'er mounds of macaroni;
They are not moved by fish and chips,
It's Islay Cheese for Tony.

Vincente Dopi — ninety-two —
Well past all thoughts of fun —
Ate half a pound and what'd he do,
But go and squeeze a nun.

The Pope has cried, 'Enough, enough,
Away with this love potion,
The wild and wanton Islay stuff,
That puts them in the notion.

I banned the Pill — a sinful curse —
- I felt their morals soar —
And now there comes a thing far worse,
This menace from Bowmore.'

Luigi Silli — eighty four —
And never termed a flirt

Went tearing out his own back door,
Chasing a mini skirt.

An old and shaking Genoese,
His pension was collectin',
Ate just one bite of Islay Cheese,
And now his wife's expectin'.

He chews a chunk and softly sighs,
'How I love this glorious Cheesa,'
Looks up aloft and loudly cries,
'Get up them stairs, Teresa.'

The old wife prays upon her knees,
'Oh Lord, restrain his sallies,
And from this awful Islay Cheese,
Protect us poor old Tallies.'

But what are the origins of the legend? Was Islay cheese ever imported to Italy? I have read a speculation that in the '50s and '60s a number of Italians may have come to Islay for fishing and shooting holidays and taken home samples of the local produce. Islay cheese may have acquired some reputation as a result. Was it ever banned? I can find no evidence of this — orders may well have been cancelled but that could have had more to do with the quality of the product.

Can cheese have aphrodisiac qualities? Apparently so; some of this may have to do with the aromas of cheese, which according to some have a vaguely sexual nature, and according to others have a more specific aroma reminiscent of the scent of a woman, though I don't advise telling your loved one that her natural scent reminds you of a powerful cheese – that is quite unlikely to lead to amative entanglements – unless she is from Georgia; it is rumoured that Georgian women have been known to pass out through heightened passion if they inhale the irresistible odour of a certain variety of local cheese. Also, according to one authority, 'The five-carbon fatty acid that gives most cheeses their flavour is a close relative to a mid-cycle vaginal pheromone.' There you go.

What about the chemical properties of cheese? Here again the evidence is supportive; cheese is known to contain ten times as much *phenyl ethylamine* (PEA) as chocolate. This substance is believed to release the same rush of hormones as sexual intercourse. This is quite separate and not to be confused with the aroma of cheese – a cheese that smells of PEA is not necessarily the best one to choose if looking for an Aphrodite door opener.

Would the Italians be aware of the magical lust lever found in certain cheeses? Absolutely! The most famous Italian seducer of all, Casanova, was said to favour the combination of red wine and stilton – if only he had progressed to Islay single malt and Islay cheese, his 'tally' could have been much higher. Furthermore a recent survey of Italian women's attitudes to foody aphrodisiacs discovered that the most

popular sex-stimulant eat treats were salami (25 per cent preferred it) and cheese (21 per cent). Of course the salami has the additional suggestive advantage of shape, but it is surprising that so many Italian women seem to agree with Casanova.

So why Islay cheese? Why should it attract the disapproval of the Pope? Is it possible that Islay cheese had some secret ingredient that pushed its priapic potency higher than parmesan or pecorino? Here are a few thoughts. Firstly, it has been suggested that cows on Islay have a higher proportion of draff in their diet than any other cows in the world. This is partly because there are so many distilleries on the island, but also because the geese eat all the grass. Draff is a solid residue by-product of whisky making and the viagric effects of whisky have been celebrated in Scotland for centuries.

Secondly, the amount of spirit evaporation (the Angels' Share) on Islay is enormous and this may have an atmospheric impact on the maturing cheese. Indeed, the Islay Creamery was established within buildings once belonging to Loch Indaal distillery and was immediately next door to warehouses containing millions of litres of maturing whisky. I have heard that some of the old style Islay cheese was matured for at least nine months so this atmospheric influence may be relevant.

Thirdly, and this is the most convincing reason for me, the old cheesemaker, John Kissock, and his son were both, according to a Port Charlotte resident I spoke to, 'legendary drinkers' and great lovers of single malt. Perhaps the secret ingredient favoured by these whisky aficionados was a splash of the good old stuff in the cheese. It might well have raised the acidity of the cheese allowing it to mature more thoroughly.

Unfortunately, perhaps due to the loss of the Italian market, the old business failed in the 1990s. Soon after, some business men and local dairy farmers got together to re-establish the Islay Creamery. Sadly that business also failed after only two years or so. I tasted the cheese, and I am not at all surprised. The level of government grants involved and the impact of the failure on the island economy meant that it became the subject of a government enquiry to establish what went wrong.

The conclusions of that enquiry referred to the fact that initially the cheese was matured too quickly and sold too young — and it seems there was little market for a mild Dunlop cheese. Once they realised this and tried to mature the cheese longer, the business plan forecasts went awry, since they had to wait longer for a saleable product. The enquiry also stated, 'Unfortunately the Cheese Company never managed to employ an experienced cheese-maker, partly due to the fact that it is not always possible to persuade people to move to an island.' Aha! So they were making cheese without a cheesemaker; one cannot imagine a distillery making a mistake like this. And, of course, they were missing the vital secret ingredient — whisky!

LEGENDARY DRINKERS

Keith Jessop became the greatest marine treasure hunter in the world in 1981 when he salvaged $100,000,000 worth of gold bullion from HMS *Edinburgh* in the Barents Sea. Keith cut his teeth on diving wrecks like the *Otranto* off the coast of Islay. In his autobiography, *Goldfinder*, he describes his time on Islay and the following quote shows he gained some insight into the social life of the island;

Islay depends almost entirely on the production of whisky and, despite the best efforts of the distillery owners, a fair amount of raw whisky, straight from the still, along with the stuff they call wash, finds its way into the hands of the locals. If whisky drinking ever became an Olympic sport, nine people out of a team of ten, including women, would come from Islay.

What about this 'raw whisky'? Is there any truth in the suggestion that the islanders drink it in vast quantities? These days, probably not; controls at the distilleries are pretty tight and distillery workers have the opportunity to buy company products at discount prices. Nonetheless, there is something indomitable in the human spirit and something creative, imaginative and deviant in human behaviour that can easily be inspired by the thought of free whisky. On the other hand people are less likely to risk their livelihoods these days, especially when it would no longer be so easy to be dismissed from one distillery and apply for a job at another. I suspect that applies both to pilfering and to being drunk on duty.

Ah! But to hear the stories that the old hands tell, is like watching old Western films full of bad lads in bad lands – bravado and fearless cheek. Also, not so long ago dramming (providing the workforce with regular drams of whisky to be drunk while on the job) was a regular feature of distillery work. I visited Ardbeg within a few days of their re-opening in 1997 and there was a slate still hanging up near the malt bins with the dram times written out in chalk. Dramming was the norm, though the regime might vary from distillery to distillery and might also vary with change of management. John MacDougall (*Wort,*

Worms and Washbacks) tells of workers dramming 'gentlemen's measures' of 15 year old malt at Laphroaig, but that may have been because it was Christmas.

Certainly, matured whisky was not the norm for dramming. Indeed, talking to people who worked in distilleries during the 1960s, 1970s and even the 1980s, 'the boys' preferred new spirit straight from the still (referred to as 'white' drams) because it had higher alcohol and therefore a bigger hit or burn. Stories are told about the boys being offered matured drams or 'goldies' (for example in the silent season, when new spirit ran out) and turning up their noses because they preferred the raw stuff. One or two of my informants have suggested that in a perverse kind of way, this was an extra, unofficial, layer of quality control. The regular drammers would soon tell the stillman if there was something not right about their tot (apart from the size that is). At a time when distilling regimes were much less tightly controlled and therefore more fickle and variable, that is almost credible.

Dramming was usually something that happened at set times in the working day or shift, but it was also a way of sweetening the pain if there were particularly hard or dirty jobs to be done. You could get distillery workers to do almost anything with the promise of an extra dram. This

widespread practice of dramming (even lorry drivers conveniently arriving just in time for the dram hand-out, would be included) must have resulted in a slightly light-headed workforce at the best of times, but there were also endless ruses devised by the boys to get their hands on new-make spirit in various unofficial ways. Everyone has stories to tell; bottles stashed in the peat stack, buckets of what looked like water being carried sloppily across the yard to dispel suspicion, holes being drilled in pipes.

And then there were the dogs! Whisky dogs are containers used for pilfering whisky from distilleries. The most common would be something like a Heinz tomato sauce bottle with a string tied around it dangling down a trouser leg. However, there were many much more imaginative, bespoke

versions, from a length of copper pipe (worn out condenser tubes, usually) with an old penny welded to the end, to elaborate devices that look like large copper hip flasks, but with curved sides so that they could be concealed under shirts and jackets. Most distillery workers, at the end of a shift, must have been walking through the gates with stiff legs, un-bending arms, stooped shoulders and funny walks – like a scene from *Invasion of the Body Snatchers*.

Speaking about body-snatchers, one of the clearest insights into the drinking style of the Ileachs is obtained by the evidence from funerals, even back to the 17th century. There exists a record of the accounts of the funeral of the fourth Campbell laird, Sir Alexander of Calder, in 1697. Items listed include 'for malt and aquavytie – £346-6/-' and for 'claret, wyne and brandie – £247-13/4'. These are incredible sums and prove firstly, that wakes were serious drinking events and secondly, that even for aristocratic wakes, the amount of whisky served far exceeded that of the more expensive imported stuff.

John MacDougall recalls that an Islay funeral could often last four days. In the context of a particular funeral reception in the White Hart, Port Ellen, he reports that a variety of whiskies were served, as well as McEwan's Export and Tartan Special for the 'teetotalers.' Whisky, being the Water of Life, is the expected thing to toast a departed friend on Islay.

I have heard people talk, with fond recollection, about the funeral of Peter Pearce of Sanaigmore. Peter was a popular guy, originally from Yorkshire, who had a passion for Islay and its whiskies. It is rumoured that he asked to be buried in the dunes at Sanaigmore and that his extensive whisky collection (some of it prizes he had won at darts and dominoes) should be employed in the old Rinns tradition of passing round drams at the graveside. All of this happened as he wished and considerable toasts to his passing were consumed by the crowd, while discussing the qualities of their departed friend and enjoying the wonderful setting of the Sanaigmore dunes. Gentle rain began to fall, and to the musical lament of James Brown's pipes, tears and rain mingled with the liquid essence of Islay making a memorable, almost legendary, funeral. It is hard to walk on the dune sand at the best of times but after that moving valediction, it is said that more than one mourner stumbled on the way down from the grave.

They say that some fabulous whisky was going around that day at Sanaigmore – certainly not the raw stuff. The days of dramming are over; probably the days of illicit whisky making are also over, but it was that tradition of secret whisky making that probably gave islanders a taste for new-make spirit in the first place. During most of the 18th century, Islay had no Excise officer and so, one can imagine there would have been considerable private and small-scale commercial distilling. The Reverend Archibald Robertson of Kildalton Parish complained about this state of affairs in the 1790s 'We have not an excise officer in the whole island. The quantity, therefore, of whisky made here is very great and the evil that follows drinking to excess of this liquor is very visible on the island... It may take some time, however, to prevent the people from drinking to excess; for bad habits are not easily overcome.' You could say he was right about that.

With the Excise Act of 1801 an officer did come to the island and within a short time there had been 233 convictions for illegal whisky making on the island. The last recorded conviction for illicit distillation was in 1850, after three men were caught at their still in a cave. Caves were popular places for whisky making; usually difficult to approach without detection and of course, out of sight. Caves reputedly used for whisky making are to be found around the Oa, particularly at Schlochd Maol Doridh, near Kintra and at Lower Killeyan (sometimes called Killean) and on the remote north shore from Gortanaoid Point to Rhuvaal. The remote coast near McArthur's Head may have housed some stills also, and it was said that there were once 10 illicit stills in Lagavulin Bay. There are many stories on Islay about the men who outwitted the excise officers.

It wasn't just the distillers, legal or otherwise, who gained notoriety for their capacity for drink. In 1824 a traveller described the noisy scene at the Port Askaig ferry and concluded that whisky did not tend to diminish the hustle and vociferation among the drovers and the boatmen. This is worthy of note because, only

six years earlier, the local Stent (Excise) Committee had been concerned with exactly this problem and sought to fix it. The notes of the Stent Committee for 1818 tell us,

It having been represented to this meeting that the Allowance of Whisky to the Ferrymen at Portaskaig has hitherto been undefined and unlimited, and a surplus quantity found often injurious to the Cattle and the proprietor thereof — Therefore it is now declared that the allowance henceforward shall be at the rate of one Mutchkin of Whisky for every 30 head of Cattle ferryed, and Mr John Hull Is authorised to restrict the quantity accordingly.

It is important to note that the whisky was not for consumption by the cattle.

This situation had not improved by 1883 when civil engineer Joseph Mitchell wrote of his experience at the Lagg Ferry at the north end of Jura (this was the commonest route for drovers taking Islay cattle to the mainland).

On arriving at the ferry we found every corner of the inn crowded with drovers who had been detained by the weather for several days, and were passing their time as was their wont, in riotous and continuous drinking. We felt it no agreeable sojourn to stay at the inn with these noisy and half-intoxicated men, for the very air was impregnated with an odour of whisky.

So they bribed the ferryman to take them over in spite of the weather but when the drovers heard of this they insisted that 18 cattle had to go too. Things got very rough in the crossing and it was a drover saved the day! 'I shall never forget the Lagg

Ferry or the gallant Highland drover, who by his prompt and decided action was the means under providence of saving our lives.' (From *Reminiscences of my life in the Highlands* by Joseph Mitchell 1883.)

John McDougall, in his memoirs, says, 'It was a way of life I had never experienced before, and I have never experienced since, and I found it quite difficult sometimes to keep my constitution in trim. Just about anything was a reason for having a ceilidh or a party.' And that, coming from a distillery manager! Many visitors to Islay have found themselves in deep trouble trying to keep up with the drinking capacity of the locals. I am reminded of Jim McEwan's story about the Japanese visitors getting so drunk at the Machrie Hotel that they didn't notice when Jim and his partner substituted a snowball for the cue ball in a drunken game of pool.

The folk that seem most likely to be targeted by the islanders for this kind of treatment, for some reason, seem to be journalists. Journalists are renowned on the mainland for their capacity for drink and so they invariably try to keep up with the islanders, usually with fatal consequences. John Grant of Glenfarclas told me a story of having been inveigled into a drinking session (again at the Machrie) with Wallace Milroy and a journalist called Allan Hall from the Sunday Times. Allan had been invited to Islay by the distilleries to write a feature on the island and its whiskies. Allan, a double target, being English as well as a journalist, was amazed at these 'generous people' constantly topping up his glass. He was on all fours by the end of the night and had to be led to his room, from whence he did not appear for two days.

The distilleries had paid for Mr Hall to come to the island and were not pleased at his early and rapid descent into incapacity. John Grant still has a letter signed by all the distillery managers telling him not to come back to the island. He says it was probably a piece of leg-pulling, but he also says that, though it was 30 years ago, he has not been back to Islay since. Neither, I think, has Allan Hall.

Tony Lord, editor of Decanter Magazine, was caught out on a similar way, in Port Ellen. Apparently, there used to be a large stuffed brown bear at the top of the stairs in the White Hart. Tony, vainly trying to keep up with the pace of dramming, had to admit defeat and stagger up the stairs. Anticipating his condition, someone had removed the light bulb and inserted the brown bear into Tony's bed. He didn't come back to Islay either; in fact he went to live in Australia. The bear was inconsolable. Incidentally, talking about bears, in one of John Francis Campbell's tales, *The Brown Bear in the Green Glen,* there is a bottle of whisky that never gets empty — a typical Islay fantasy.

POEM: ISLAY MIST

This is the man
Going home from the inns:
A pocket full of nothing
Roaming through the Rhinns.
Lost in the Islay mist
Where no-one can find him
Leaving his future and
His footmarks behind him...
No one can see him

And nothing can he see
Neither his wellingtons
Nor his own knee.
Can't see his hand
Can't see his wrist
All for the sake of
The Islay mist.

from *Cladville Cakes* (*Songs from the Rhinns*) by
Lennart Hellsing

MURDER MOST FOUL

Murder is not a common crime on Islay, in fact crime of any kind is relatively rare. However, over the years the island has seen the occasional murder committed; in most cases drink has been implicated one way or the other. A murder might happen in a major city anywhere in the world and few people would even hear of it. On Islay, the whole island is scandalized and everyone talks about it and it can easily become part of the orally transmitted folklore.

Murder at Mulindry

It was during the long feud between Angus Macdonald of Islay and Sir Lachlan Mor Maclean of Duart Castle on Mull that the legendary feast at Mulindry took place. These guys would have made Billy the Kid, Ghengis Khan and Hagar the Horrible look like 12 year old ballet dancers.

Maclean was a larger-than-life fellow who brought trouble wherever he went. In 1588 a galleon from the Spanish Armada strayed into Tobermory Bay. It wasn't long before Maclean was involved with the Spanish, trying to recruit them as mercenaries for his inter clan battles. Some say he became romantically involved with a beautiful Contessa who was on board. The story goes that his wife found out and was not chuffed, so she had a consultation with the blue witch of Lochaber and they came up with a revenge scheme that involved blowing the Spanish galleon to smithereens. Believe what you like, but the Spanish galleon did blow up and a few bits still lie in Tobermory Bay.

Lachlan finally met his end in 1598 at the Battle of Traigh Gruinart on Islay. This time it was he who consulted a witch before heading off to battle, but with typical high-handed arrogance disregarded

every bit of advice she gave him and ended up being killed by an arrow from the bow of a black fairy dwarf from Jura. This black fairy, or *dubh sith*, was a mercenary working for Angus Macdonald's son James; he had originally offered his services to Lachlan but his offer got the same overconfident rejection as the witch's advice. Even in death, Maclean caused trouble. While his body was being carted by his aunt to Kilchoman for burial, his feet were dangling over the end of the cart, jumping

about like a dancing wooden doll as it bumped on the rutted track. This made his aunt's dimwit son Duncan laugh out loud; the aunt thought this such an insult and sacrilege that she stabbed her own son to death on the spot. A cairn to commemorate the happy event stands there to this day.

Anyway, to back-track a few years, the feud between Angus and Lachlan had reached outrageous heights of idiocy with body parts hacked off and heads flying, like a scene out of a Monty Python sketch. Even the King (James VI), who was not averse to a bit of gore and mayhem himself, eventually got fed up and told them to sort it out – or else. In typical fashion of those who are obsessed by a family feud, they went through the motions of seeking peace, while neither actually believed a word of it. It was a dynastic game of chess – planning moves and strategically jostling for the upper hand.

So, they appeared to shake hands and

bury the hatchet. Lachlan acknowledged Angus as his overlord regarding his land holding on Islay (the Rinns) and Angus even sent his young son James to live with Lachlan for a while, as a gesture of goodwill but probably hoping he could spy on the enemy, seemingly unaware that babysitters are not always to be trusted. The two parties and their entourages met for a big reconciliation feast at Duart, which ended up as a six day spree of overindulgence and intoxification involving 'gluttonie and drinking without all measure.' Unfortunately, at some point in the happy get together a drunken bard started singing snidey songs about the McConnells, who were distantly related to, or allied with, the Macdonalds and this got up Angus's nose.

Angus was too clever to be openly outraged on the enemy's home ground and instead contained and disguised his anger, plotting revenge instead. After an appropriate time had passed, Angus invited the Macleans over to Islay for the second leg of the world drinking and gluttonie contest. This time it took place at Mulindry – not even a castle, more of a farm steading. In fact Lachlan had a castle on Loch Gorm but it had been blasted to bits in a siege back in the 1570s, this being part of the background to the feud. After only one night of drunken revelry (Macleans 6 – Macdonalds 1), the Macleans were given lodging in a building that had been used as a kiln. One can imagine rows of drunken Macleans snoring away on the upper floor of a maltkiln, the place full of heavy aromas of peat-reek and vomit.

Probably Angus could have arranged a sort of knock-out contest whereby the bards tried to out-slag each other and may the best bard win, but by this time he had nursed his wrath too long and only total annihilation would do. In the middle of the night 200 of his men surrounded the kiln and perhaps started singing songs that were slightly disrespectful to the outnumbered Duart Macleans. Lachlan himself was invited with mischievous glee to join Angus for a night cap or 'final drink'. He was smart enough to take the young James with him, in fact wearing him on his back as a kind of human chain mail.

Angus appeared for the friendly drink, swaying in the doorway with a bottle in one hand and a large sword in the other, clearly intending that the last drink of the night would be short and swift. It was young James who called out to his father to be reasonable and pleaded for mercy on behalf of Lachlan, to whom he had become attached, not just by being strapped to his back. This was the same James Macdonald who later would try to burn his father out of his own house in sheer frustrated annoyance with the old feller and who would give the black fairy dwarf of Jura permission to shoot an arrow through Lachlan's skull; but for now he was young and squeamish.

Now, the next thing that happened was that a rumour came to Islay that the perfidious Macleans had done in Angus's brother Ranald, so the Macdonalds proceeded to murder two Macleans a day. The poor Macleans soon found they had more than hangovers to cope with. This went on for some time until Lachlan was about the only one left. Then word came that the rumour was false and Ranald was alive and well. Angus grudgingly let Lachlan go. He should have finished him off because anyone could tell that the feud was not going to end there.

Indeed it rumbled on until the fateful day when the *dubh sith* of Jura, hidden up a tree, aimed his arrow at the back of Lachan's head while he unwisely drank from the well of strange Neill, again ignoring the specific advice of his witch consultant.

The point of this story, I suppose, is to show how much trouble can result when drunken bards are allowed to unleash the true weapons of mass destruction – satirical songs.

Incidentally, after the Battle of Traigh Gruinart, the fleeing Macleans got the same treatment again when they closed themselves inside a church for sanctuary. The Macdonalds burned the lot of them – and the church – but that doesn't count as murder because it was classed as an actual battle.

Murder at Ellister

A rather grizzly double murder happened at Ellister in 1698. A bunch of no-goods, including brother and sister Donald and Efferick McKenzie, John McVeir (Efferick's husband), Christian McMillan (wife of Donald) and Katherine McIndughlassie murdered Moir NcIlchenich, a widow at Ellister, for her money. One doesn't imagine they wanted the widow's money to buy shoes or lottery tickets – they were after drink. Poor Moir was strangled with a belt and her body flung into the sea.

A lengthy drinking spree then no doubt took place, but it appears that the parties fell out when the maudlin Christian McMillan began to feel remorse and blubbered about confessing the deed to the authorities. Before anybody had the chance to sober up, McVeir (who one now assumes was the owner of the belt that strangled Moir) decided that the blabbermouth McMillan had to go the same way as the widow. The exact transcript of the trial says

> that he did upon a day in the previous September unknown, with force and violence cast and throw one Christian McMillan the wife of Donald McKenzie in Ellister over a rock at the Ellister shore, where they had gone to collect shellfish, into the deep sea where she was immediately drowned and died.

Presumably he managed this while holding up his trousers with one hand.

Now Donald was slightly attached to his wife (not literally, of course, or he would have drowned too) and so this deed, instead of shutting the group up, had them all immediately racing to the authorities and grassing on McVeir. The authorities arranged two separate trials at Inveraray and hanged the lot of them. Incidentally one of the jurors at the trial of McVeir was a maltman.

Murder at Kilchoman

On Monday 15 December 1823, John McLergan, a 54 year old labouring man from Connisby, was having a dram in a public house at Kilchoman. He was in the company of friends, William McQueen and the Gillespies of Gorteninlost among others. They had just attended the funeral of Catherine McLergan, an elderly unmarried woman to whom John was related. They were probably lamenting the passing of the old woman and warming themselves after standing in the cold while she had been laid in the grave.

Suddenly, the saloon door was kicked open and three ruffians sauntered in. These were brothers Donald and Alex Currie and Donald Niven. They had a grudge, though one gets the feeling that any imagined or invented grudge would be enough to rile these characters up. The Curries had had some malt whisky seized by the Excise and for some reason they thought that McLergan and his cronies were to blame and they were insisting on a compensation payment from McLergan, who naturally had refused to pay. They announced that they had already given the other loathsome creatures at the table their punishment and now it was the turn of McLergan.

They pounced on him and dragged him outside and proceeded to give him a thorough kicking. McLergan tried to escape his vicious attackers but one of them pursued him and struck him hard on the head with a large stone. He was left in a severely beaten state and was eventually helped home by his friends from the pub. John languished in his bed for almost a week but died from his wounds the following Sunday.

He was examined by a surgeon by the

name of Neil Currie (no relation to the attackers, one might assume) who found 'a deep and dangerous cut on the top of John's head, apparently inflicted by some blunt instrument, such as a stone or piece of hard wood.' He also had nine wounds on his face, which was badly inflamed. Currie considered him to be 'in a dangerous state.' However, he was able to describe what had happened to him, though he could not be sure which of the attackers had hit him with the stone.

As soon as it was known that McLergan had died of his wounds, Donald Currie, conscious of his guilt, bolted and left the island. However, he was apprehended and imprisoned at Inveraray Jail. Records show that he was sentenced to seven years transportation, being sent firstly to the prison hulk *Retribution* on 12 June 1824 and then transferred to the *Sir Charles Forbes* on 16 November, for the voyage to Van Diemen's Land. It is not clear what his ultimate fate was.

Murder at Port Ellen

According to a Womens' Rural Institute book about Islay, there was a folk belief that blood stains which could not be washed away were a sign that murder had been committed. Not far from Port Ellen locals knew of a spot where there were three brown spots or bloodstains. At that exact location, a young man, the only son of a widow, had been murdered by two men. These men had discovered a keg of spirits and killed the young man because he was a witness and might inform the Excise men.

STOLEN WHISKY

In 1999 Morrison Bowmore sent Jim McEwan, Global Brand Ambassador, to Canada to promote their whisky. Jim, always the showman, organized (with considerable publicity) the most expensive whisky tasting ever, in the Seven Seas Restaurant in Vancouver. The whole thing was staged as a publicity stunt, with the press being leaked a story that the bartender at the restaurant had purchased one of the most expensive whiskies in the world – the 40 year old Bowmore – at £4,000 (about $8,000 Canadian) a bottle.

Jim arrived dressed in a kilt, surrounded by guys in suits wearing shades – like *Men in Black* agents. The whisky arrived separately in a Brinks armoured jeep. Tickets for the dinner and whisky tasting at the Seven Seas were sold for $1,000 each. The press were skilfully reeled in and Bowmore got the publicity they wanted.

A couple of days later they got even more publicity when a bottle of the fabulous 40 year old Bowmore, which had been on prominent display in the ritzy Chateau Louis liquor store in Edmonton, was stolen. I was in Canada at the time and even as far away as Ontario this was big news. The national newspapers, TV and radio were all covering the story of the hi-jacked bottle no. 249.

The story ran and ran when it emerged that the whisky kidnappers were demanding a ransom of $2,500 for the return of the celebrity bottle. Negotiations were attempted but before Bowmore could decide whether to pay or not, the trail ran cold. Either the thieves considered the tricky nature of a ransom exchange too risky for a mere bottle of Scotch – or they got fed up waiting and drank it. Well, I am sure they drank it anyway; it seems unlikely that it is in some gangster's whisky collection somewhere – more likely it was unceremoniously scoffed, possibly resulting in the most expensive hangover ever. No-one knows the fate of the ransomed Bowmore 40 year old.

I had the good fortune to taste some of this marvellous 40 year old at Whisky Live in Tokyo a few years ago. It is without question a fabulous whisky, in which the usual smoky flavours of Bowmore have given way to exotic fruits through long maturity (Jim McEwan says that some of the Bowmore warehouses, so close to the sea, are perfect for long, slow maturation).

I was also with Jamie MacKenzie, a couple of years ago, when he delivered the last available bottle of 40 year old to the Widder Bar in Zürich. This was to go on sale over the bar at a phenomenal price. I asked the bar manager, Markus Blattner, if he thought it would sell. He answered that it would sell within a year and that he was confident he would make a profit – in fact, I heard later, it sold within a month. The 40 year old is also on sale in the Louis Bar of the Art Deco Hotel Montana in Luzern. The proprietor there is Fritz Erni who has the largest collection of Black Bowmores in the world – he served me a dram of Black Bowmore once – but that is another story.

With a whisky of this age, of course, the nose and flavour are only part of the experience. It is impossible to ignore the emotional aspect of drinking a whisky that was made so long ago. Jim also tells of an experience in the USA, on that same promotional trip on which the 40 year old was stolen, when a man in the audience broke down in tears. The whisky had taken him back to the '60s and his experience in Vietnam. He had been the sole survivor of a bomb blast that killed his three buddies. The Bowmore had reminded him that he had not fulfilled a promise he made to visit the Veterans Memorial in Washington every year. After his confessional in the whisky tasting, he was determined to put it right.

The 40 year old Bowmore stolen in Canada was not the only memorable theft of whisky from this most unfortunate distillery. On 4 December 2007, a shipment of Bowmore whisky was taken in a bold, broad daylight heist. 10,000 bottles of Bowmore worth £300,000, and intended for the Christmas whisky market, were stolen from an independent haulier in Hertfordshire. The thieves persuaded the Dutch lorry driver (who had limited English) waiting to unload his cargo into the bonded warehouse in Hoddesdon, that due to a problem with the fork lift truck, he should follow them and unload his stuff into another warehouse in nearby Waltham Abbey instead. Presumably there were howls of laughter as their lorry sped off to a riotous party that evening, and some professional criminals had large, clinking stockings that Christmas.

Barely two months earlier, Bowmore made the record books with the sale of the most expensive whisky ever bought at auction. A 157 year old (there's emotion for you) had sold at McTear's for £29,400, even though the cork had collapsed into the bottle. Unfortunately the private, anonymous purchaser was easily able to outbid Morrison Bowmore who wanted the whisky that they had made back on display in the distillery. Ah well, you win some, you lose some. Maybe the successful bidder drank the whisky and was so disappointed that he (or she) had the lorry load of Bowmore stolen to satisfy his (or her) honour.

Here are the words of a song I wrote about the lovely town of Bowmore and its fabulous whisky. The song was recorded on my third whisky album *One for the Road* (CDTRAX313)

REACHING HOME

The sun is warm, the air is clear and still
Soon we'll be standing on the pier
They chased the devil from the church on the hill
And they offer you angels' tears
I never knew the name
Of the angel who flew too close to the flame
And maybe, maybe,
Maybe I never will

The sun is climbing high overhead
The distance fading from the view
A wisp of smoke is a homespun thread
Through silver and gold and blue
It comes as no surprise
That all these years under foreign skies
Has made me, made me,
Made me lose the thread

CHORUS

You can come in the night
Like a silkie from the sea
Eyes quick and bright
Full of destiny
Or like a broken king
In the hour before the dawn
Hoping to find your Avalon
Sun on the water makes you feel you can fly
Smoke on the water makes you cry
Smoke on the water makes you cry

Dusk is here and far in the west
Soon the fire will be gone
Reaching home is the hardest test
With the **darkest** night coming on

The ship of **legend** turns
And the **mariner** knows the sweetness
   that burns
And says he, says he,
Says he'll return at **dawn**

You can come in the night
Like a silkie from the sea
Eyes quick and bright
Full of destiny
Or like a broken king
In the hour before the dawn
Hoping to find your Avalon
Sun on the water makes you feel you can fly
Smoke on the water makes you cry
Smoke on the water makes you cry

THE BOWMORE LADE

Water is a crucial part of whisky making. After unusually dry spells in the spring of 2003 and again in the early summer of 2008 a number of distilleries on Islay had to stop production due to lack of water. Distilleries are very careful to look after their water sources, whether from lochans, streams or boreholes. Water quality is obviously crucial, but equally important is the fact that they need a lot of it, not just for process but also for cooling.

Bowmore is unique on Islay for having a water source that is delivered by a lade (a man-made mini canal). Indeed it has the longest lade of any distillery in Scotland. The Bowmore lade is said (by the distillery and by Andrew Jefford, who has walked it) to be 14 kilometres (nine miles) in length, diverting water from the Laggan River away up past Mulindry. The lade has a drop of only about 30 metres (100 feet) over its whole length and was built 4ft wide and 4ft deep.

The Bowmore lade was constructed in the mid 19th century when the distillery was owned by the Mutter family of Glasgow. Details of its construction are obscure; it is said to have been constructed by a squad of Irish 'navvies' (short for navigators). It is a significant feat of engineering. Some sections have a gradient so slight that the lade can seem, like the Electric Brae, to be running uphill. Legend has it that a local tailor was consulted in the engineering of these sections and that he helped the navvies achieve the finest of gradients by running drops of water down a slender, taut thread.

There is a whiff of scandal about this in the writing of an Exciseman on Islay at that time, John Murdoch, who suggested that the Mutters had persuaded the inspector of the Relief Committee to provide funds towards the building of the Bowmore Lade. Murdoch, a radical land reformer, was of the opinion that the Relief Committee's responsibility was towards the poor of the island and that the proprietors of the distillery should have paid for the lade themselves. However, it is possible that the lade construction was an attempt to provide some employment for impoverished islanders and that the Mutters and the Relief Committee had joined forces in this job creation scheme. That does not quite fit with the folk memory that Irish navvies were brought in and the story will have to remain a mystery for now.

In the old days, one of the jobs that needed to be done in the silent summer season, when production stopped and maintenance was of primary concern, was for men to go out from Bowmore Distillery to clear the lade. It would take a squad of six men four weeks to complete and was dirty, difficult, midge, cleg and tick-infested work, done with spades, scythes, edging tools and wheelbarrows. Nowadays, most of the lade can be cleared by machine, though the folk wisdom among distillery workers is that the first time the lade was cleared by mechanical digger, it made it too wide, which limited the flow and for the first time ever, water supply became an issue.

There is, however, one section of the lade that cannot be cleared by machine — the area in the Tallant Wood is a protected, conservation area and in any case access is difficult. This area still needs to be cleared by hand in the traditional way. Back in the 1960s and '70s it was considered to be one of the dirtiest jobs and as such required particularly good dramming as reward. Future archaeologists might find a puzzle when their excavations turn up an unusual number of discarded whisky bottles, all bearing the same company logo, in the idyllic surroundings of the Tallant Wood.

THE KILDALTON CROSS

The Great or 'High' Cross of Kildalton is an extremely important Celtic cross and may be Islay's most remarkable historical artefact. Dating from around 800AD it stands nine feet high and is made of one large slab of grey-green epidiorite rock quarried nearby, close to Ardmore Point. The sculptor, probably from Iona, has created a cross that is slightly asymmetrical, probably due to following the grain of the rock.

The carvings on the cross are quite remarkable, and although suffering from considerable weathering, most of the scenes depicted (and their symbolism) can still be made out. Recurring motifs of angels and serpents (worms), along with the proximity to Ardbeg distillery, suggest references to whisky making. However, the main theme of the cross is that of sacrifice, which is represented in various scenes.

One scene depicts Cain murdering Abel. The two brothers had made a sacrifice to God. Cain, the tiller of the soil, gave fruit and vegetables, while Abel, the tender of flocks offered the blood of an unblemished lamb. God accepted the lamb but turned up his nose at the vegetables, which made Cain angry and annoyed so he beat his brother to death with the jawbone of an ass.

Another scene depicts Abraham about to sacrifice his only son Isaac, at God's request. Now biblical scholars draw parallels between the 'sacrifice' of Isaac and God's sacrifice of his only son, Jesus. However, there is also a parallel with the famous Celtic story of the old man who sacrificed his son to protect the secrets of the heather ale – a story wonderfully re-told in Robert Louis Stevenson's poem *Heather Ale*.

In 1882 the cross, which was leaning at an angle, was removed to allow repair to the foundations. During the excavation of the cross, human remains were found underneath it. Apparently the bones were those of a person who had been ritually tortured and sacrificed in very gruesome way, usually described as 'the blood eagle'. The victim would be spread-eagled or pinned face down on the ground, their ribs then cut near the spine and pulled back, resembling blood-stained wings. The victim's heart and lungs were then ripped out from the back and held aloft. Apparently this was a popular sport of the Vikings, usually reserved for someone considered to be of important status or particularly brave.

The name Kildalton apparently means 'the church of the foster-child', with the reference probably being to St John the Evangelist. St John, one of the 12 disciples of Jesus, is usually depicted in Christian art with an eagle and a chalice. The chalice could refer to the legend that at the Last Supper he was handed a chalice of poisoned wine, which he blessed, causing the poison to rise out of the cup in the shape of a serpent. Alternatively, it could signify the words of Jesus to John (and John's brother James) 'My chalice indeed you shall drink' (Matthew 20:23).

Angels and worms, symbols and sacrifice – the plot thickens. I am no Dan

Brown, but I think it is highly likely that the Kildalton Cross commemorates the abbot of a monastery who refused to tell the Vikings were the whisky was hidden.

The Box of Bones

Ardbeg is not the only distillery to have a connection with the discovery of human remains. There follows a report from the *Oban Times* around 1881.

> Port Askaig — Curious Find — At Bunnahabhain, where a new distillery is in process or erection, the following singular incident occurred a few weeks ago: - While one of the gentlemen in superintendence over the building was walking on the margin of a moor skirting the bay, he became thirsty, and, searching for water, lit upon what appeared a promising but confined spring. Judge of his surprise, when, on stooping to widen the aperture, his hand partially uncovered a small box with a loose lid, which, when raised, revealed the strange spectacle of a number of human bones blackened with age, and mouldering in decay. Several other parties were immediately called to the spot, but none knew anything about the apparently clandestine burial; conjecture was utterly at fault. On making enquiry in this neighbourhood, the only likely explanation we can find is to the effect that about 20 years ago the box and its contents were deposited in their present resting place by a sea-captain, now deceased, and that the human remains were anatomical studies, used by his relative, a doctor, who had gone abroad, leaving behind him this singular legacy.

'Anatomical studies' indeed; nowadays, speculators would immediately cast around for more sinister and salacious explanations, but for now, this has to remain just one more of the island's mysteries.

THE LITTLE OLD MAN WITH THE SACK OF GRAIN

A little old man was walking from Ballygrant to Port Ellen with a sack of barley. It was a journey he had done many times before, but this time he was feeling very tired and after a few miles the sack seemed very heavy indeed. He stopped at a croft and asked the crofter if he would look after the sack for him while he went off for a rest. He wandered off onto the moor to find a sleeping spot. The sun was warm and he soon fell asleep and seemed to sleep right through to the next day.

Once awake he went back for his sack of grain, but when he got there he was told by the crofter that the hen had eaten all his grain in the night. The little old man picked up the hen, stuffed it in his bag and continued on his way.

After a few hours he grew tired again and stopped at another house, where he asked if they would keep an eye on his hen while he took a nap. He went off to find a dry spot on the peat bog and slept soundly. When he returned for his hen he was told that the crofter's cow had sat on the hen by mistake, and killed her. The little old man tied a rope around the cow's neck and took her with him on the next leg of his journey.

The cow slowed him considerably, and, after a few hours he grew tired again, this time asking a farmer if he would look after the cow while he had a sleep. Once more, he slept soundly and went to collect the cow in the morning. He was told that the farmer's daughter had taken the cow to the river for a drink but it had slipped on the ice, broken a leg, and had to be put down. The little old man picked up the farmer's daughter and put her in his sack.

This time the going was really slow. Eventually he came to an inn and, leaving the sack against a wall outside, went inside for some refreshment. While he was having a dram or two, the farmer, who had

been following him, let his daughter out of the sack, replaced her with some stones and tied it up again.

When the little old man eventually picked up his sack to continue his journey he found it to be even heavier than before. He continued on for a few miles, sweating profusely and cursing the whisky for making him so weary. Eventually, he could carry on no more and, crossing a bridge, threw the sack with its contents into a deep pool in the stream. Then he turned and headed back down the road for home, grumbling and empty-handed.

THE LOST DISTILLERIES

Islay is the whisky island and it has a fine range of distilleries concentrated in a small area but it once had more; names that are whispered now and again, evoking an age now long gone. The 18th century was the great age of distillery building and on Islay this was largely a time of transition from farm distilleries to larger units. Some have faded from the folk memory more than others. What do we know about these legendary distilleries?

Killarow

There are no distilleries around Bridgend these days (though there is a brewery) but in the past there may have been three. The oldest was a distillery run by David Simson at Killarow up to 1766, when he closed it, moved to Bowmore, and established the distillery that is now the oldest on the island. In the 1760s Daniel the Younger had the whole settlement at Killarow moved to Bowmore in order to create spacious parklands around Islay House. I guess the distillery had to be swept away along with everything else.

Bridgend

There seems to have been a distillery called Bridgend, built by Donald McEachern in 1818. It may have operated single distillation but it did not last long and was apparently wound up in 1821. However, J. MacFarlane registered a distillery in Bridgend in 1821. It is not clear whether this is the same one.

Daill

The McEachern family also opened a distillery at Daill Farm, near Bridgend, in 1814. Initially registered to Neil McEachern, it passed to Malcolm McEachern in 1825 and a year later the licence was held by Donald McEachern, who operated the distillery until its demise around 1830. Some of the buildings at present-day Daill Farm may be remnants.

Newton

Newton, on the road out of Bridgend towards Ballygrant had a distillery which was established by Thomas Pattison. Some sources say it was started in 1819 and others in 1825. It operated until 1837 when it finally closed. This Thomas Pattison may have been the father of the one who translated Gaelic poetry and who composed the poem of *Captain Gorrie's Ride* (see page 135). Some possible traces of this distillery are still to be seen at Newton House.

Scarrabus

A little way further along the road to Ballygrant you can turn off to Scarrabus, where a licence to distil was taken out by John Darroch & Co in 1817. This establishment lasted only two years.

Mulindry

Also short-lived was a distillery situated on the River Laggan near Mulindry. It operated from 1826 to 1831 and was water powered. The owner was John Sinclair, who was reputed to be too fond of the cratur himself and lost the distillery through bankruptcy, following which he emigrated to America.

Lossit

A distillery was established at Lossit, near Ballygrant (not to be confused with Lossit Beach on the Rinns) in 1826. It seems to have functioned continuously, though under different ownership regimes, until the 1860s, by which time it appears the distillery was closed, although the warehouses continued to be used by Bulloch Lade & Co, who owned Caol Ila distillery. Some traces may survive near Lossit Kennels.

Ardmore

There have been other distilleries situated on Lagavulin Bay. One was established in 1817 (the year after Lagavulin distillery) by Archibald Campbell. It was sometimes referred to as Ardmore and sometimes as Lagavulin No 2, particularly after it was taken over by John Johnston of Lagavulin distillery. For a while the two distilleries were operated in harness but eventually Ardmore was swallowed up by what is now Lagavulin.

Malt Mill

Malt Mill was a distillery built in a huff. Peter Mackie of White Horse Distillers, owned Lagavulin and had the sales agency for Laphroaig. When the owners of Laphroaig decided to award the sales contract to someone else in 1907, 'Restless' Peter got a bit agitated and built Malt Mill in the grounds of Lagavulin in a fit of pique. He wanted to make a Laphroaig style of whisky of his own.

Unfortunately, though he copied Laphroaig's equipment and recipe, and even poached some of the staff, it never quite matched the peatiness of Laphroaig. Nonetheless, it operated until the 1960s when it was eventually merged with Lagavulin. The reception centre at Lagavulin was once part of Malt Mill.

Ardenistiel

There have also been two distilleries at Laphroaig. The other was known as Ardenistiel (or sometimes Kildalton or Islay distillery). This distillery was financed by the Gairdners, with a lease granted by the Laird, Walter Fredrick Campbell; it was operated by Andrew and James Stein. There were frequent quarrels between Ardenistiel and Laphroaig, usually over water rights. The Steins gave up in 1846, when Andrew died and James went to work at Port Ellen. The man who took over Ardenistiel was John Morrison, who had done spectacularly badly at Port Ellen distillery; he did the same here. It was taken over a year later by William Hunter, who gave it a few years of courageous effort but the new laird, John Ramsay eventually invited Dugald Johnston to take Ardenistiel over as part of Laphroaig some time in the 1860s.

Tallant

Tallant is a farm not far from Bowmore, near the Laggan Bridge. A distillery was set up there in 1821 by brothers John and Donald Johnston. It was always a small-scale operation though it stayed in production until 1852. The Johnston family were to become significant players in the development of Laphroaig.

Octomore

Moving round to the Rinns, there used to be a distillery at Octomore Farm. Octomore is a beautiful spot above Port Charlotte with wonderful views to Ireland and to the Paps of Jura, as well as the rest of Islay. This is where Dirty Dotty's Well, a spring of pure water running off the ancient rocks of the Rinns, is to be found; a blessing for any distillery. Octomore ran from 1816 to 1840 under the control of the Montgomery family. It was built by George Montgomery, whose gravestone can still be seen at Bridgend; he initially ran it in partnership with his father, John, and one other.

Unfortunately, the short history of Octomore distillery is one of family fights over inheritance rights and ownership squabbles relating both to the distillery and the farm land. The 1840s were a time of over-population and famine on Islay. The population at Octomore then was 175 people in 30 houses, 27 of whom were Montgomeries, but that declined steadily through emigration so that a decade later there were only 51 people in 10 houses. By 1854 all the Octomore Montgomeries had died or emigrated and the distillery, in ruins, was acquired by the new Laird of Islay, Charles Morrison.

Now there are five people in one house at Octomore, but you can rent a holiday cottage that is a renovation of part of the old distillery. A whisky called Octomore has recently been produced by Bruichladdich distillery. It is the most highly peated malt ever made and was named after this defunct distillery at Octomore Farm.

Lochindaal

Also in Port Charlotte, Lochindaal Distillery (aka Port Charlotte distillery) was established in 1829 by Colin Campbell. It had various owners subsequently, the last being the Distillers Company who acquired it in 1929 and closed it down, wiping away a hundred years of distillation. Apart from Port Ellen, it is the only lost distillery on Islay that we have a description of from Alfred Barnard. That is illuminating; Barnard makes it clear that 'peat only is used in firing the malt' so it would have been a smoky beast. He tells us that some of the whisky was shipped out from Bruichladdich Pier and 'the remainder floated out to the ships, 10 casks being lashed together by iron pins and a chain called 'dogs,' and towed out by boatmen.' There are echoes here of the Beast of Scantcastle (see page 88)

I have seen a bottle of Lochindaal whisky in the collection of Claudio Bernasconi in St Moritz, Switzerland but such bottles must be extremely rare. Many parts of the buildings survived; some are presently used by Bruichladdich as warehouses, others became the Youth Hostel or the Islay Natural History Centre and at one time the Islay Creamery. The owners of Bruichladdich distillery now have plans to rebuild Lochindaal Distillery. They have also produced a whisky of medium peating which they called Port Charlotte.

Port Ellen

Port Ellen distillery was closed in 1983. It had survived from its inception in 1825, though it was mothballed between 1929 (the same year Lochindaal was closed) and 1967, when it was rebuilt. There is still some Port Ellen malt available, though it is naturally becoming increasingly rare and is being snapped up by collectors. I believe some of the buildings survive within the complex of the Port Ellen Maltings though I suspect that the plant is gone. Neil Wilson, in *Scotch and Water*, records that the malting floor was once used as a mortuary, when the dreadful disaster of the *Otranto* resulted in many bodies being swept ashore around the Oa.

This was a distillery of historical significance (the spirit safe was invented or pioneered here) and its produce is very highly thought of. One cannot help thinking that a blink of vision, a weak pulse of enthusiasm and a modicum of investment could see Port Ellen resurrected, even on a small scale. The whisky market is very buoyant at the moment; new distilleries of every conceivable scale are being built and old ones resurrected. Could there be someone in Diageo with a creative, romantic inclination and the ability to imagine not-entirely-commercial possibilities? Islay would rejoice!

THE MacBEATHS OF KILCHOMAN

Whisky expert Alex Kraaijeveld has developed the MacBeatha hypothesis. In essence it runs like this; the family MacBeatha (other forms include MacBeth and Beaton) were for centuries the hereditary physicians of the Isles (indeed of Scotland for a long time). He says there is some evidence that the MacBeatha family name first appeared in the late 13th century when Angus Og, Lord of the Isles married Agnes an aristocratic lady from Ulster. Agnes brought with her a number of Irish people of skill and learning, believing that her new home of Islay would benefit from such a civilizing influence. Among these was a healer called MacBeatha.

Tradition has it that the MacBeatha family settled in Kilchoman on the Rinns of Islay. There is certainly hard evidence in the form of a cross at Kilchoman commemorating the MacBeathas. Alex Kraaijeveld speculates that the MacBeathas brought the secrets of distillation from Ireland to Scotland. If so, says Kraaijeveld, then Kilchoman is the 'cradle of distilling in Scotland.' Not surprisingly, this thesis is to be found on the wall at the new Kilchoman distillery. Kraaijeveld also speculates that *uisge beatha* might actually mean 'the water of MacBeatha' rather than 'the water of life.' (An equally logical version is that MacBeatha means 'son of life' – perhaps a name given to someone whose father was unknown.)

Certainly there is no dispute about the eventual hereditary status of the Macbeatha or Beaton family as the physicians to the Lords of the Isles and the Scottish Kings. Records show Fergus McBeath was physician to King James VI in 1609. Fergus is supposed to have cured the King of scrofula, often referred to as 'the King's Evil,' though this seems to be a reversal of a European-wide tradition that scrofula was called the King's Evil because Kings were supposed to have the ability to cure their subjects of the disease by the royal touch.

There is no question that there was a connection between a branch of the MacBeatha family and Kilchoman. The cross has already been mentioned and records show that a Beaton who was physician to the Lords of the Isles held land 'at Ballinabe, Areset, Howe and Saligo.' There may be a problem with the timing, however. Patrick MacBeth was the principal physician to King Robert I (The Bruce) in 1308 and that seems like a rapid rise in a short space of time from being one of the retinue brought to Islay by Agnes just a few years earlier.

Furthermore didn't Scotland have a King called Macbeth back in the 11th century? In fact the family of that Macbeth came from Moray, another ancient centre of distilling. I have argued elsewhere that Shakespeare's Macbeth did not really meet with three witches round a cauldron on Knock Hill near Alves in Moray, but instead with three monks and their mashing vessel, making this perhaps the earliest account of whisky making in English literature.

I have no doubt at all that the early healers in Islay and the rest of Scotland would have been held in high esteem and repute if they had *aqua vitae* in their medicine bags. Is whisky not 'the cure for which there is no disease'? The Scots always understood this. Even the English understood it eventually — there follows a quotation from Raphael Holinshed's *Chronicles of England, Scotland and Ireland* (1577) about the curative powers of whisky; (incidentally the same Holinshed from whom Shakespeare got the historical background for his play *Macbeth*!)

> Being moderately taken it sloweth age, it strengtheneth youth, it cutteth fleume, it lighteneth the mynd, it quickeneth the spirits, it cureth the hydropsie, it healeth the strangulation, it pounceth the stone, it repelleth gravel, it puffeth away ventositie, it kepyth and preserveth the head from whirlying, the eyes from dazelying, the tongue from lispying, the teeth from chatterying, the throte from rattlying, the weasan from stieflying, the stomach from womblying, the harte from swellying, the bellie from wirtching, the guts from rumblying, the hands from shivering, the sinews from shrinkying, the veynes from crumplying, the bones from akying, the marrow from soakying, and truly it is a sovereign liquor if it be orderlie taken.

The Irish monks, on the other hand, were reputed to use whisky as 'an embrocation for sick mules' not really grasping its potential. Incidentally, if the MacBeaths came from Ireland, why is it such a rare surname in Ireland now? In Scotland it has flourished but in Ireland the guys with the fabulous elixir — the sons of life — have faded away. I don't think so. The more you

examine this question about which way the whisky travelled the more you have to question the MacBeatha hypothesis. The Irish themselves claim that it was their patron saint, Patrick, who taught them the secrets of whisky distilling. Experts seem to agree that Patrick was actually born near Dumbarton but was captured in his youth and sent to Ireland as a slave. If he had learned whisky making in Scotland and demonstrated his ability to the Irish — no wonder he was transformed from a slave into a saint!

Whisky as medicine has a long tradition on Islay and the other islands. No-one is at all surprised that Laphroaig was the only whisky to beat prohibition in America — because it was classed as medicinal. Tobias Smollet (also born near Dumbarton) reported in his novel *The Expedition of Humphrey Clinker* that the local people gave their children whisky to protect them against smallpox. It seems to have been quite efficacious because there were no smallpox epidemics recorded in the Hebrides. Of course liver disease may have been endemic, the records are not clear.

I heard many stories on Islay about the famous Doctor Archie. This was Archie MacKinnon who was a Port Ellen GP in the 1970s. Archie was himself a legendary drinker who only drank triple measures; to quote one Islay character I spoke to, 'Archie was aye pickled!' John MacDougall wrote of him, 'Archie's idea of a dram was to fill a tumbler to the brim with whisky and then ask you if you took anything in it.' Apparently his abiding philosophy was that very few ailments would not respond to the healing combination of whisky and time. Many locals would appear at Dr Archie's house of an evening complaining of this or that and he would dispense 'medicine' from his cabinet. As well as a well-stocked whisky cabinet, Dr Archie also developed his own special recipe for an elixir or potion that of course included whisky, though no-one is quite sure what else was in it. No doubt it provided protection against the weather and all the ills of life, and of course, evidence that the spirit of the MacBeaths of Kilchoman persists.

UISQUEBAUGH BAUL

Martin Martin (in Gaelic Màrtainn MacGilleMhàrtainn) wrote *A Description of the Western Isles of Scotland* published in 1703. Martin was born on the Isle of Skye and so had enough familiarity with gaeldom that his accounts can be taken as reasonably reliable. He makes reference to whisky as it was made on the Isle of Lewis in the 1690s, as follows;

Their plenty of corn was such, as disposed the natives to brew several sorts of liquors, as common usquebaugh, another called trestarig, id est, aquavitæ, three times distilled, which is strong and hot; a third sort is four times distilled, and this by the natives is called usquebaugh-baul, id est, usquebaugh, which at first taste affects all the members of the body: two spoonfuls of this last liquor is a sufficient dose; and if any man exceed this, it would presently stop his breath, and endanger his life. The trestarig and usquebaugh-baul, are both made of oats.

Well, things have changed since the end of the 17th century. Only recently is whisky being made again on Lewis though it is not quite ready yet. They say that, in Scotland, the best whisky is made in the inner isles but consumed in the outer isles. Those who do make whisky on the islands, use only malted barley. The maverick distillers of Bruichladdich have not yet ventured into making oat whisky though they have made it using bere barley, and a fine dram it is too. They were also inspired by Martin Martin's account of *trestarig* and *usquebaugh baul* to have a go at making those.

Jim MacEwan and Mark Reynier invited me to the distillery in February 2006 to witness the first attempt at creating four-times distilled single malt. I watched and waited with Jim McEwan and stillman Neil MacTaggart as the stills slowly came to temperature, the butterfly flap in the spirit safe started to tremble and at last the fabulous, four-times distilled spirit started to run. At various stages, after the foreshots had run, Jim took samples and he and I made comments on the character, nose and taste of the mighty new spirit. The final strength of the new spirit was 89.9% abv. Jim's tasting notes eventually went like this;

The whisky first ran at 92% down to 88% which will make an average of about 90%. It is very similar to the whisky tasted by Martin all those years ago. On entry the flavour is cool, fizzy, citrus – lemon and honey, then the taste of soft gooseberry and pear in syrup evolves as it glides across the palette with cereal and toasted muffins in the slipstream. There is no evidence of the power at this stage because the viscosity is almost like glycerine, however as it engages the taste receptors at the back of the tongue it really hits the booster button and an amazing heat floods deep into the chest. It's brilliantly fresh and fizzy with an extremely pleasant afterburner effect and leaves an aftertaste that is superb, not long but unforgettable – believe me.

I remember *The Sun* and the BBC both sent a reporter and a photographer. The next day *The Sun* had photographs of their reporter breathing fire after consuming two spoonfuls of *usquebaugh baul* – in other words they treated it as a bit of fun. The BBC, on the other hand, had coverage of the item on the evening television news which included an interview with a spokesperson from Alcohol Concern, who considered Bruichladdich's behaviour irresponsible. That may possibly be true if they were to sell the stuff at natural strength, which is extremely unlikely. In fact, *uisquebaugh baul* is slightly less powerful than grain whisky, which runs off the column stills at 94.5% abv. Perhaps the man from Alcohol Concern was not aware of that.

They may not sell it at natural strength, but they did give souvenir bottles of the new spirit, with *uisquebaugh baul* labels signed by Mark Reynier, to the guys from *The Sun*, from the BBC and myself. Sadly, the busy reporters, flying back to the mainland had their souvenirs taken from them at the airport because it was too high in alcohol to be allowed on a plane. Being a penniless songwriter, I went back on the ferry and Calmac don't really care what you have in your rucksack, so I still have my bottle. I also spent my time on the leisurely crossing from Port Askaig to Kennacraig writing a song about *uisquebaugh baul*; the lyrics are below.

In the May 2007 Islay Festival, Jim McEwan served a very young sample of Uisquebaugh Baul at his masterclass in the distillery. It had been matured in a bloodtub and even at a few months old it was a stunning dram. Jim offered an opinion that the high alcohol content had drawn character from the cask much more quickly than ordinary fillings. Perhaps this was the secret of rapid maturation. The following year, in May 2008, the distillery Valinch offered for sale was X4 + I *Deliverance*; not yet whisky, but highly drinkable and the name, X4 and the alcoholic strength at 65.4% abv give clues to how the stuff will eventually appear on the market once it has passed its statutory three years.

At the end of 2008 Bruichladdich released very fancy packages of X4 new spirit bottled at 50% abv. It seems this limited release is aimed at the curious, the collector and the 'mixologist'. Fair enough, but I am patiently waiting for the matured stuff. 54 casks of American White Oak were filled so it will appear on the market, when Jim and Mark consider the time is right. Some of it will be left to mature for its maximum term, in other words until it drops to 40% abv due to the angel's share. Whisky this strong could still be viable in 80 years time – no need to bury this in the earth or wrap it in cling-film!

TV's wine expert Oz Clarke and *Top Gear*'s James May attempted to run a high performance racing car fueled by this 'high octane' single malt whisky, as part of *Oz and James drink to Britain*, broadcast on BBC2. The Radical SR4 racing car was filled after Oz had tasted the stuff. Then, on a closed off road near Blackrock at the head of Loch Indaal, carefully cleared of sheep and cattle – the car managed an impressive 0–60 mph in 3.5 seconds. Apparently the main problem was steering it in a straight line – a case where the car and not the driver ought to be breathalysed!

James May, more of a beer drinker, had a minor road-to-Damascus conversion in that programme; standing with Mark Reynier and Jim McEwan in the

Bruichladdich warehouse, tasting the X4, he said,

> That's remarkable! That is an exceptionally exciting whisky drinking experience. Whisky normally takes me to a dark place – like a windowless bothy on a dark night with the rain outside. It's a last refuge – beyond that, all hope is lost; it will either take you into the abyss or release you from it. But this is one of those moments of great clarity of thought – you put it on your tongue and there's a moment when you see all the Jesus light coming through the sky and the clouds parting – the rain lifting – and all those things. It's very brief; but it's there!

Any drink that can inspire such eloquence and elation AND improve the weather should definitely be available on the NHS.

Uisquebaugh Baul

CHORUS
Uisquebaugh Baul, Uisquebaugh Baul
High intensity alcohol
Exceedingly risky
It's perilous whisky
One sip and you'll stumble and fall

Uisquebaugh Baul is four times distilled
Some say it cures and some say it kills
Take my advice and make out a will
Before you try Uisquebaugh Baul

Take one sip but don't take a second
It packs more punch than ever you reckoned
You'll spin in the wind like the Corryvrekkan
With dangerous Uisquebaugh Baul

CHORUS
Uisquebaugh Baul, Uisquebaugh Baul
High intensity alcohol
Exceedingly risky
It's perilous whisky
One sip and you'll stumble and fall

The island of Islay has numerous wrecks
Mostly from flinging it over their necks
And now here's a dram that's better than sex
Four times Uisquebaugh Baul

This is the stuff to put out your lights
It kicks, it bites; it's like kryptonite
You can lie on the floor but you have to hold tight
For you're spinning with Uisquebaugh Baul

CHORUS
Uisquebaugh Baul, Uisquebaugh Baul
High intensity alcohol
Exceedingly risky
It's perilous whisky
One sip and you'll stumble and fall

One spoonful your heart's beating fast
Two spoonfuls you're feeling quite gassed
Three spoonfuls you've breathed your last
You're in the past – Oh, What a blast –
*   Uisquebaugh Baul*

Uisquebaugh Baul, Uisquebaugh Baul
High Intensity, Seventeenth Century,
Savage ferocity, super velocity
Wonderful Uisquebaugh Baul

This song is on *One for the Road* (CDTRAX313)

SECTION TWO

THE WHISKY ISLAND

LAST TANGO IN PORTNAHAVEN

Andrew Jefford, in his book on Islay and her whiskies (*Peat Smoke and Spirit*), described the shape of the island as one resembling a witch. I look at the map and see another possibility – the two parts of the island are dancers twirling each other around in a *ceilidh* dance, like in the cross-handed birl of a Strip the Willow. The main part of Islay is the larger, more muscular, younger partner, while the Rinns is the smaller, older, more lightweight but wiry dancer being swept off its feet. Drawing four feet onto the outline of the island will show what I mean.

The southern half of the Rinns is made up of the oldest rocks on Islay and among the oldest in Scotland. These Gneiss rocks were formed under the crust of the earth about 1,800 million years ago, long, long before there was any life on the planet, and since then, what we now know as the Rinns of Islay has been involved in a fascinating slow dance of land forms and continents that has seen it move from near the South Pole in a meandering zigzag to its present position.

About 700 million years ago, the Rinns was attached to the coast of a continent called Gondwanaland, facing another continent, Laurentia across the narrow Dalriadan sea. Whimsically, as the narrow sea began to widen into the Iapetus Ocean, the Rinns broke away from Gondwanaland, kissing goodbye to what would eventually become part of South America. It changed partners and attached itself to the coast of Laurentia, which drifted northwards, eventually to become most of North America and Greenland.

About 480 million years ago, the Iapetus Ocean closed again and the three continents of Laurentia, Baltica and Avalonia clashed together. Like a Dashing White Sergeant, land masses came up to each other, with an almost audible 'Heyeeuch!' and then parted again. It was around this time that Scotland crashed into England and the Rinns snuggled up to the rest of Islay. As the partners parted again, the Rinns stayed with Islay and Scotland but waved goodbye to Laurentia which drifted away on the other side of the growing chasm of the Atlantic Ocean.

So the Rinns of Islay has danced its way across the surface of the globe, at various times cheek to cheek with South America, North America and Europe. Hanging on to the extreme western edge of Europe now, it looks like it might be keen to change partners again!

This scenario explains why the Rinns is barely attached to Islay (the neck of land between Loch Indaal and Loch Gruinart is little more than sand dunes), why its rocks and topography (and therefore its agriculture and its people) are subtly different from the rest of Islay and why the folk of the Rinns are, if not the best dancers, at least the most enthusiastic (something I can vouch for having attended dances in Portnahaven and Bruichladdich). It also explains the strange affinity that exists between the Rinns of Islay and Arequipa, Peru.

That a portion of Islay might once have

been joined to Peru is mind-boggling enough, though the evidence is there in the rocks. When it turns out that part of Arequipa is called Islay, spelled and pronounced in the same way, the coincidence either makes your brain ache or you guffaw in your beer. But in a stranger than fiction reality, it is absolutely true. It seems impossible that the Spanish language would have produced such a name, and improbable that native Indian tongues would have either. The people of Islay, Arequipa say that the name came from a settlement named after an ancient Inca tribe called Risla. Risla became

anglicised in the 18th or 19th century by immigrant miners and railway workers. This seems unlikely — where did the 'y' come from? Another theory is that some Victorian geologist may have applied the name after realising the similarity between the rock formations; who knows?

Whatever the reason, Mark Reynier, Managing Director of Bruichladdich, when he discovered this, immediately invited the Mayor of Islay, Peru to attend the Islay Festival in 2007, as a special guest of Bruichladdich distillery. Miguel Ramon, accompanied by his aide and interpreter, Victor Garcia-Belaunde, made a very favourable impression on their Scottish hosts, rising to the serious events with statesman-like presentations and yet being quite capable of intensive partying also.

I accompanied M. Reynier and M. Ramon from Bruichladdich to Wester Ellister for an informal dinner and witnessed a rather bizarre moment of serendipity. M. Ramon had been presented with a kilt which he wore with some panache and in return he made a gift of a poncho to M. Reynier. M. Reynier could easily have passed for Clint Eastwood in a spaghetti western, if it hadn't been for the Peruvian woolly hat with dangly lugs. On the way, the convoy passed between fields inhabited by Highland cows on one side and Alpacas on the other. Only on the

I PREFER BERGMAN OR FELLINI, MYSELF..

Rinns could something like this have happened without being staged. Looks were exchanged but no-one said anything.

It is unlikely that the Rinns of Islay will suddenly swap *ceilidh* dancing for mambo, salsa and the cha-cha-cha, but a detectable change in its dance floor performance has been noted. While Bruichladdich was closed the folk of the Rinns were slowed down to a slightly depressed shuffle but in recent years Bruichladdich has opened again, proving to be an economic stimulus to the whole area. Now there is a new distillery at Kilchoman and plans to re-establish Lochindaal distillery in Port Charlotte. Suddenly one senses a lightness in the step, almost a cocky swagger and the traditional half bottle of whisky is back, swinging in the jacket pocket.

LOGANAIR FLIGHT LC423

At twenty past three in the afternoon of 12 June 1986, a Loganair scheduled flight from Glasgow was approaching Islay with 16 people on board. It was a de Havilland Twin Otter 300. The weather was not very great – wind of five knots, very low cloud and heavy drizzle. The co-pilot was at the controls, as he was working through a programme of supervised training having recently changed to flying the Twin Otter. The designated commander was in the co-pilot's position.

The plane had reached the south shore of Islay and was flying parallel to the coast towards Port Ellen at a low altitude. At three twenty-one the Islay airport gave them a weather update which they acknowledged, replying that they were over Port Ellen. In fact they were not over Port Ellen but over Laphroaig. Visibility was so poor that the less experienced man at the controls mistook the lights of Laphroaig for those of Port Ellen and turned the plane to the right, thinking he was heading for the airport. In fact he was heading for some very rough and rocky high ground. One minute later the plane crashed.

In the words of the official investigation,

In conditions of low cloud and poor visibility, the pilots mis-identified Laphroaig as being Port Ellen and very shortly after turning inland the aircraft struck rising ground approximately one nautical mile from the coast at a height of 360 feet above mean sea level.

The pilot saw the ground approaching and tried desperately to climb. This proved sadly impossible, but the fact that the plane hit the ground at a rising angle allowed it to slide uphill some way before crashing into rocks and that may account for the survival of the passengers.

Amazingly, none of the passengers was killed, though 11 were injured. As the plane crashed however, one wing broke and turned inward; the still spinning propeller sliced through the cockpit, killing the handling pilot instantly. The supervising pilot sustained serious injuries to his head and legs and could not afterwards remember anything about the flight or the crash. At the subsequent inquiry the cause of the crash was given as 'The commander's decision to allow the handling pilot to carry out a visual approach in totally unsuitable meteorological conditions. An error in visual navigation was a contributory factor.'

A number of local people were quickly on their way to the scene, including the Port Ellen doctor, Archie MacKinnon, who had to be carried up the hill due to his age, size and state of health. The exact place where the plane crashed is shown on the OS map as Borracheil, which incidentally is the same name given to the fairy mound in some of the gaelic tales (see The Legend of the Smith and the Fairies, page 127) and for whatever reason, local whispering has it that though the passengers were undoubtedly lucky to survive the crash, in nearly every case bad fortune has followed them since.

Is this another case, like at least three of the Fleetwood trawlers and the Chappex yacht, (see page 72) of a distillery luring vessels and passengers, siren-like, to misfortune?

60

TEN SONGWRITERS ON THE ISLAY WHISKY TRAIL

In 2002, Jim McEwan invited me and nine other members of the Lanarkshire Songwriters Group to Islay for a long weekend. The primary purpose of the trip was to have fun; the secondary purpose was to write new songs about Islay. In fact the group eventually produced 22 songs. Bruichladdich paid the costs of transport and accommodation, which was in three of the chalets at the Machrie Hotel. They also arranged for numerous field visits, including for example, a visit to Finlaggan and a peat-cutting session with Norrie Campbell.

The song writers performed two concerts, one in Portnahaven Hall and one in Bruichladdich Hall. The song writers had beers in the bus, drinks on the ferry, arrived at the Machrie Hotel to find bottles of whisky on the table in each chalet and of course had to have an in depth visit to Bruichladdich distillery. Some of the poor creatures were not used to such sustained bouts of merrymaking and there were one or two mild casualties over the weekend, including John Malcolm and Dave Gibb, both of whom wrote songs about the legendary trip, which is still talked about with affectionate memories by those who were involved. Jim McKenna, the only member of the group who doesn't drink (any more) is a taxi driver by profession and the obvious choice to be the designated driver. He doesn't hang around on the road.

TEN SONG WRITERS ON THE ISLAY WHISKY TRAIL

By John Malcolm

Ten song writers on the Islay whisky trail
Ten song writers on the Islay whisky trail
When one song writer missed the ferry sail
There were nine song writers on the Islay whisky trail

Nine song writers on the Islay whisky trail
Nine song writers on the Islay whisky trail
And when one song writer fell over the gang plank rail
There were eight song writers on the Islay whisky trail

Eight song writers on the Islay whisky trail
Eight song writers on the Islay whisky trail
And when one song writer ended up in jail
There were seven song writers on the Islay whisky trail

Seven song writers on the Islay whisky trail
Seven song writers on the Islay whisky trail
And when one song writer went the other song
  writer's bail
There were six song writers on the Islay whisky
  trail

Six song writers on the Islay whisky trail
Six song writers on the Islay whisky trail
And when one song writer's liver began to fail
There were five song writers on the Islay
  whisky trail

Five song writers on the Islay whisky trail
Five song writers on the Islay whisky trail
And when one song writer started to feel frail
There were four song writers on the Islay
  whisky trail

Four song writers on the Islay whisky trail
Four song writers on the Islay whisky trail
And when one song writer found he had to
  read in braille
There were three song writers on the Islay
  whisky trail

Three song writers on the Islay whisky trail
Three song writers on the Islay whisky trail
And when one song writer said he should have
  stuck to ale
There were two song writers on the Islay
  whisky trail

Two song writers on the Islay whisky trail
Two song writers on the Islay whisky trail
And when one song writer turned a whiter
  shade of pale
There was only Jim McKenna left to tell the
  tale

THE LANARKSHIRE SONGWRITERS
VISIT TO ISLAY
By Dave Gibb

An outing for songwriters on a twenty seater bus
Jim McKenna's at the wheel he says — 'It's
  Islay boys or bust
Because there's nothing going to stop us and if
  there's some who think they can
Then we'll run right ower the tap o' them and
  turn them into Jam'

Well we sped past Inveraray and we made it
to the boat
When this woman with a ruler raised her
hand and shouted 'Stop!'
Well she measured us and told us we were two
feet over long
We had to pay an extra sixty quid before
they'd let us on

CHORUS

There were bunny rabbits, squirrels there were
foxes frogs and toads
There were cows and sheep and cyclists and
the odd wee nanny goat
They were diving into thickets; they were
jumping out the road
Cause the big white bus was heading up to Islay

Well we made it to the Machrie where the
rooms were nice and neat
We also found some Bruichladdich that we
swallowed down a treat
Now whisky's fine in moderation as I'm sure
you all know well
But if you gulp it down like water it can make
you feel quite ill

In the morning I am trying hard to get out of
my bed
I'm not sure what's spinning round — is it the
room or just my head
So after boaking at my breakfast we decide its
time to go
So we climb into the big white bus and head
along the road

CHORUS

There were bunny rabbits, squirrels there were
foxes frogs and toads
There were cows and sheep and cyclists and
the odd wee nanny goat
They were diving into thickets; they were
jumping out the road
Cause the big white bus was heading up to Islay

Digging peat with Stormin' Norman on a
bleak and windy plain
He is really quite a man — his patter's some-
thing else again
At least the fresh air clears away the pain
inside my head
But then we're set upon by midges and that's a
fate that's worse than death

Because the Islay midge is a mighty midge — a
truly fearful thing
For the Islay midge has hobnailed boots and
carbon fibre wings
It spies its prey at forty yards and sets out to
attack
It sees a flabby pale-skinned tourist and it
thinks — 'I'm having that!'

CHORUS

There were bunny rabbits, squirrels there were
foxes frogs and toads
There were cows and sheep and cyclists and
the odd wee nanny goat
They were diving into thickets; they were
jumping out the road
Cause the big white bus was heading up to Islay

A trip round Bruichladdich where the whisky
    is distilled
Jim McEwan poured us whiskies just to give us
    all a thrill
He said — 'You'll have to try this clear stuff
    that has only just been made'
Well I felt my tongue explode as both eyes flew
    right out my head

When I recovered my composure and felt that
    I could see again
We headed for the concert where we were to
    entertain
All the locals who had been so kind and taken
    time to come
And it must be said we went down well and
    everyone had fun

CHORUS

There were bunny rabbits, squirrels there were
    foxes frogs and toads
There were cows and sheep and cyclists and
    the odd wee nanny goat
They were diving into thickets; they were
    jumping out the road
Cause the big white bus was heading up to Islay

When the trip was over and it was time to
    head for home
We nearly missed the ferry cause the big bus
    widnae go
But an islander with jump leads helped to get
    us on our way
And with Big Jim at the wheel it wasn't long
    till we were hame

A weekend to remember — cracking drink and
    folk and food
And I didn't throw up on the ferry as I really
    thought I would
The people were so kind they always shook us
    by the hand
And finished off each sentence with — you'll
    have another dram

CHORUS

There were bunny rabbits, squirrels there were
    foxes frogs and toads
There were cows and sheep and cyclists and
    the odd wee nanny goat
They were diving into thickets; they were
    jumping out the road
Cause the big white bus was heading up to Islay

The island quakes in its boots at the
thought of a return visit from the
Lanarkshire Songwriters — once their livers
have recovered.

THE *EXMOUTH OF NEWCASTLE*

One of the most harrowing of the stories from Islay's past is that of the wreck of the *Exmouth of Newcastle*. The *Exmouth* was an emigrant ship, sailing from Londonderry to Canada in 1847 with a crew of 10 and 241 passengers, mostly women and children (72 were children under the age of 14); emigrants fleeing the Irish famine and hoping to start a new life in Quebec.

On the second day out from Derry, a terrible storm arose which severely damaged the ship. Captain Isaac Booth decided to turn before the storm and head back east in the hope of finding a haven for repairs. Eventually a crew member spotted a light; Booth, thinking it was the Tory Island light, ordered the mate to steer a course slightly to the north of it, believing he would be in open water. Then came the horrible realisation that instead of a steady light, it was a flashing light, and therefore had to be the Orsay light at the south end of the Rinns of Islay. Booth's navigational reckoning was mistaken by about 100 miles, not so surprising considering the weather conditions, and so the *Exmouth* was heading for the rocky coast of Islay.

Booth and his crew made frantic efforts to steer the ship further to the north, away from the shore but the storm had a hold of the ship and there was just not enough room to manoeuvre her out of danger. Shortly after midnight, in the dark rage of the storm, the *Exmouth* was driven onto the rocks at Geodha Ghille Mhòire. So wild was the sea that within minutes the vessel was ground to pieces on the black rocks. Three of the crew were able to clamber along a fallen mast that lay briefly against the rocks. Apart from these three, there were no survivors.

The thought of all these poor souls, including so many children and infants, trapped in the crowded hold, after three days of frightful weather and being tossed around on a heaving, angry sea, is one that pains the heart. Perhaps, when the sea finally blasted the *Exmouth* to pieces, death was in some way a release from their suffering.

It is hard to see a whisky connection in this story, except that one of the islanders who played an important role in trying to recover bodies from the sea, and who left us a written account of what he witnessed, was John Murdoch, HM Excise officer to the island. Murdoch later became well-known as a radical thinker, land reformer and temperance supporter; he was jointly responsible, along with Keir Hardie, for establishing the Scottish Labour Party. Excise officers have seldom occupied heroic roles in the folklore of Scotland, so this is worthy of note.

Another who played a part in the horrible aftermath of the *Exmouth* tragedy was John Francis Campbell, who also drew sketches of the scenes, 'recovering bodies at Geodha Ghille Mhòire' and of the 'burials at Traigh Bhàn'. Thus the man who would later collect so many Gaelic tales found himself, for a few days, a participant in one of the most gut-wrenching of Islay's stories.

The author Joe Wiggins tells the Exmouth story in his book *The Exmouth of Newcastle 1811 –1847*. Wiggins was active in organising a memorial monument to recall the tragedy. That memorial monument now stands near Sanaigmore and there is another smaller stone at Traigh Bhàn.

In a ceremony to unveil the monument in June 2000 a group of people from Ireland came to Islay. According to Wiggins' booklet there was an evening reception and ceilidh at which 'toasts were generously donated by Ardbeg, Lagavulin, Bowmore, Caol Ila and Bunnahabhain distilleries in Islay and Bushmills distillery in Ireland'. It is comforting to see that the traditional Islay approach to wakes can still step up to the mark, even 160 years after the people died.

THE LEGEND OF THE *MAID OF ISLAY*

Legend has it that on a calm summer's evening in 1837 the Devil visited the church in Bowmore. The famous and unusual 'round church' of Bowmore was built that shape so that the Devil could find no corners to hide in. In case you are wondering why he would waste his time in the church when there is a distillery down the hill, I should explain that the church was built in 1769 – 10 years before the distillery, so they were probably quite wise.

Anyway, needless to say, the congregation spotted the Devil (or Auld Nick as he is sometimes known in Scotland) and these were not the kind of people to be won over by his tempting offers so they chased him out of the church. He fled down the hill to the distillery where there are plenty of corners, but the angry congregation quickly followed, hoping to confront the great enemy. The distillery gates were slammed shut to prevent the Devil from escaping and the entire place was searched from the malt barns to the mash house. The Devil was not to be found.

Now, just about the same time, some night workers were loading casks of Bowmore whisky onto the *Maid of Islay* – a small paddle steamer used for transporting whisky to the mainland. As darkness fell, the *Maid of Islay*, finally loaded, gave a loud blast of her horn and paddled off across the calm waters of Loch Indaal for the mainland. They never did find the Devil and the legend now says that he must have escaped inside one of the casks of whisky. Certainly he would have been terrified and desperate to escape from a crowd of angry Presbyterians and all the angels that float around the distillery.

The *Maid of Islay* also disappeared that night and no-one knows what happened to her, but occasionally, on calm evenings, distillery workers hear a noise that could just be the sea lapping against the distillery walls but it definitely sounds like a paddle steamer out on the loch. This, they believe, is the ghost of the *Maid of Islay*.

The reason, they say, is that the Devil developed a taste for Bowmore whisky and is very keen to return; he comes close but dare not land because of the fright he got last time. In fact he stays away from Islay altogether and that is why none of the nasty evil things that happen on the mainland ever occur here – an oasis completely free from sin and mischief of any kind. As Jim McEwan likes to say – 4,000 people and only one policeman! Hardly even a prosecution for drinking and driving (but see page 151).

Black Bowmore

So the Devil's favourite whisky is Bowmore and of course his very special favourite is Black Bowmore. These days he runs a rather swanky joint in Switzerland, right under Mount Pilatus (where dragons dwell and where the bones of Pontius Pilate are buried) and is an avid collector of Black Bowmores. He showed me his collection once and we even shared a wee dram of BB, which according to Andrew Jefford 'makes the knees of those who have tasted it knock in recollection'. As I watched him sensually sipping his dram, immaculately dressed in black apart from a red tie, which dangled like a serpent's tongue, I could see how he might persuade some people to sell their souls.

THE *TRUE BLOODED YANKEE*

One December night in 1813, an enemy warship stole into Loch Indaal and caused some consternation among the people of Bowmore. According to a communication from an Excise officer at Bowmore distillery to his father in Glasgow, the warship the *True Blooded Yankee* burned a number of ships in the harbour and fired cannon into the town; many of the townsfolk fled into the hills.

Records show that the *True Blooded Yankee* was in fact originally the British Navy brig-sloop *Challenger*. In 1811, while under the command of Goddard Blennerhassett, she was captured near Roscoff, in the English Channel, in a fog by two French frigates. On his release from French captivity, Blennerhassett was court-martialled but acquitted, the loss of the ship being attributed to the top masts being shot away.

Once under the control of the French, *Challenger* was sold to an American merchant living in Paris by the name of Henry Preble (Henry was the younger brother of Edward Preble, the US Commodore).

Challenger was re-fitted and re-named the *True Blooded Yankee*. A letter of marque was acquired, granting permission to operate the vessel as an American privateer and from early 1813 it sailed out of two or three French ports, mainly Brest, under the command of Captain Thomas Oxnard

The *True Blooded Yankee* was one of the fastest ships afloat, carrying 18 heavy guns and a crew of 180 men. She caused considerable trouble and alarm up and down the west coast of the British Isles. In her first few days out she captured the English merchant ship *Integrity* with its cargo of 2,200 barrels of grain (and that's a lot of potential whisky!). She then sailed to Bergen with her prize; the King of Norway

ordered her out of Bergen within eight days, but nonetheless bought the cargo of grain at a very reasonable price.

The records show that on one cruise lasting 37 days the *True Blooded Yankee* 'captured 27 vessels, held an island off the coast of Ireland and burned seven vessels in a harbour in Scotland.' This was the episode described by the Exciseman to his father. It was also reported in the *Glasgow Herald* on 10 December, the writer claiming that the *Helena*, sloop of war under the command of Captain Montressor had immediately sailed to Islay in response to the reports, but had arrived three days too late. Montressor then sailed north through the Sound of Mull in unsuccessful pursuit.

In fact, the *True Blooded Yankee* was finally recaptured a few months later by Royal Navy vessel *Hope* under the command of a young Captain named James Weddell. This is the same man who later as a seal-hunting 'scientist' gave his name to the Weddell Sea in Antarctica. His father was a Presbyterian upholsterer from Dalserf in the Clyde Valley.

The short-lived but devastating reign of terror caused by the *True Blooded Yankee* in 1813 left its mark on the folk memory of the island of Islay. Cannon balls allegedly from the warship are still on display in the Port Charlotte Museum. Sir Walter Scott, on a trip in the company of lighthouse builder Robert Stevenson (grandfather of the novelist) in 1814, had a bit of a fright when a ship sighted on the horizon was feared might be an American privateer. The Stevensons incidentally completed the Orsay (Rinns of Islay) lighthouse in 1824.

There is a story on Islay that the *True Blooded Yankee* took on board a miller from Ardnish (Nerabus) effectively kidnapping him and forced him to help pilot the ship into the inner waters of Loch Indaal. When Islayman Donald Connel died in 1985, his obituary in the Oban Times claimed that his great, great grandfather, Neil Connel, had been taken prisoner by John Paul Jones. This seems to be a confusion. John Paul Jones was reported to have visited the area in 1778 when he intercepted the Islay packet and robbed a certain Major Campbell of Islay of a fortune (see page 154); the Loch Indaal incident is quite separate.

Author, Robert Storey, was intrigued to find that Robert Louis Stevenson's unfinished novel, *St Ives*, had chapter headings sketched in for the unwritten chapters, such as 'The East Wind Blows' and 'The *True Blooded Yankee*.' Storey recognised the reference to the historical incident in which the ship of that name attacked Bowmore and he went to Islay to do further research. He realised that Stevenson had intended to tie this true story into his novel.

St Ives was finished in 1897, five years after Stevenson's death, by Arthur Quiller-Couch. Quiller-Couch had the hero, St Ives, escape southwards from Edinburgh by balloon, but Storey realised the direction was wrong. In 1990 Jenni Calder was commissioned by publisher Richard Drew to complete Stevenson's tale in line with his original intentions.

So now there is a legend which ties the strange facts of history with the imagination of R. L. Stevenson and the finishing touches of Jenni Calder. It goes like this: During the Napoleonic wars, a French soldier who had been imprisoned in Edinburgh Castle, made a daring escape to evade recapture by jumping aboard a hot air balloon. The balloon was carried westward by the wind and finally came down in Loch Indaal where the Frenchman and the balloonist were rescued by the miller of Ardnish and his son.

Almost immediately all four were taken aboard the *True Blooded Yankee*. St Ives was treated reasonably favourably as France and America were allies and he was sent ashore to warn the population. He spoke with the Exciseman at Bowmore distillery. He then had to find his way round the shore, through Bruichladdich and Port Charlotte to get to Ardnish where he knew the Captain intended to drop the miller off. He was finally able to re-board the ship and sail with her back to France and to freedom.

The book is a great adventure tale in the true tradition of Robert Louis Stevenson's stories. Jenni Calder also visited Islay to conduct some research and stayed with Mr and Mrs McTaggart at Kintra. Their daughter Iseabail is currently Operations Manager at Bowmore distillery and it is the *St Ives* story that features on one of the now very collectable Bowmore Legend tins. Jenni Calder's father was David Daiches, a prolific writer who wrote three books about whisky and four about Robert Louis Stevenson. Little surprise then, that in the Jenni Calder version of *St Ives* there is the following exchange;

> **Captain Oxnard** — 'Islay. A pleasant place, so I'm told. I hear they distil a fine liquor and I much look forward to tasting it. Ours will be a brief visit, but my intention is to linger long enough to visit the distillery at Bowmore.'

St Ives — 'I have not had the pleasure of a visit, though I own if I had known Islay's reputation for whisky I might have made a point of it. Whisky is one of the few contributions Scotland has made to civilization — indeed, I believe one may find more enlightenment in a glass of usquebaugh than in the great intellects of Edinburgh. Only the beauty of Scotland's women rivals the influence of her whisky.'

Captain Oxnard — 'Good whisky and beautiful women! I regret even more that, on this visit at least, there will be little time to enjoy either.'

THE WRECK OF THE *MARY ANN*

The story of the wreck of the *Mary Ann* in 1859 is in some ways an Islay version of Whisky Galore and the wreck of the SS *Politician* near Eriskay. In the case of the *Politician* the cargo of spirits was so large that the locals had to focus on getting it hidden from the authorities. With the *Mary Ann*, the beachcombing salvagers had no thought but how to consume the loot on the spot. Because of this, unhappy consequences followed. The story could not be told more eloquently than in the newspaper article which follows (it appeared in the *Greenock Advertiser* of 27 May 1859).

Disgraceful wrecking scenes at Islay

THE BRIG *Mary Ann*, of Greenock, now lying a wreck at Kilchoman Bay, Islay, is fast breaking up and portions of the cargo floating ashore.

Up to Saturday there had been about 200 boxes saved, containing bottled brandy, whisky and gin, and upwards of six puncheons of whisky, brandy and wine; but the wildest scenes of drunkenness and riot that can be imagined took place.

Fishermen

Hundreds of people flocked from all parts of the neighbourhood, especially the Portnahaven fishermen, who turned out to a man.

Boxes were seized as soon as they were landed, broken up, and the contents carried away and drunk.

Numbers could be seen here and there lying amongst the rocks, unable to move, while others were fighting like savages.

Sergeant James Kennedy and Constable Colin Chisholm, of the County Police, were in attendance, and used every means in their power to stop the work of pillage.

Disapproval

They succeeded in keeping some order during the day of Thursday, but when night came on the natives showed evident symptoms of their disapproval of the police being there at all, and on the latter preventing a fellow from knocking the end out of a puncheon, in order, as he said, to 'treat all hands', they were immediately seized upon by the mob and a hand-to-hand fight ensued, which lasted half-an-hour, and ended in defeat for the police of whom there were only two against the 30 to 40 of the natives.

Retreat

The police beat a retreat to Coull farm — about a mile from the scene of the action — closely pursued by about 30 of the natives, yelling like savages.

Mrs Simpson of Coull, on seeing the state of matters, took the police into the house and secured the doors, at the same time placing arms at their disposal for their protection. The mob yelled two or three times round the house, but learning the police had firearms, they left and returned to the beach.

Frightful

Next morning the scene presented was still more frightful to contemplate.

In one place there lay stretched the dead body of a large and powerful man, Donald MacPhayden, a fisherman from Portnahaven, who was considered the strongest man in Islay; but the brandy proved to be still stronger. He has left a wife and family.

Others apparently in a dying state were being conveyed to the nearest houses, where every means were used to save life.

Remedy

Mrs Simpson, who is a very kind and humane person, supplied every remedy, but there was no medical man within 15 or 16 miles of the place.

Mr James Simpson got a coffin made for McPhayden and had him interred on Friday.

At the time when the corpse was being taken away, some groups could be seen fighting, others dancing, and others craving for drink, in order, as they said, to bury the man decently.

Up to Saturday there was only one death, but it was reported on Monday that two more had died.

Cargo

The *Mary Ann* had onboard 300 tonnes of pig iron, a large quantity of spirits, and other general cargo, from Glasgow to New Brunswick.

Shortly after going to sea she became leaky, put to Dublin, where she discharged, and got repaired.

Abandoned

Going to sea again, she sprang a leak off the west coast of Islay, the wind blowing fresh off the land; and Captain Pryce, finding the vessel in a sinking state and quite unmanageable, along with the crew, abandoned the vessel.

The wind veering round to the westward, a fisherman picked her up and ran into Kilchoman Bay, where she sank in shallow water.

Donald McPhayden's death notice gives the cause of death as 'intoxication'.

THE *WYRE MAJESTIC*

Of the many ships that have come to grief around the coast of Islay, *Wyre Majestic* is the most visible, at the present time, though she shares the fate of all wrecks and is slowly being consumed by the sea. She grounded on rocks at Rubha a' Mhill, near Bunnhabhain distillery, while she was 'westering home' (a little poetic licence there) to Fleetwood. Surely she is evidence of the siren power a coastal distillery can exhort on thirsty seamen.

In fact, whisky probably was involved in a slightly different way in the demise of *Wyre Majestic*. I have pieced the story together from various website sources, so unfortunately cannot guarantee the truth of everything that follows, but then we are dealing with whisky legends.

Wyre Majestic and her sister ship *Wyre Defence* were returning from a very successful fishing trip, somewhere off the west coast of Scotland. They were both trawlers based in Fleetwood, Lancashire (the Wyre is the river that runs through Fleetwood). It was October 1974 and both vessels arrived in Oban with their large catch of fish and the crew proceeded to celebrate their success in traditional trawlerman fashion, involving lots of alcohol.

Oban harbour, however, was very busy, and the Fleetwood trawlers were unable to secure a berth. They decided, therefore on a change of plans and left Oban on the evening tide, heading for home. Just before 10 o'clock at night they entered the Sound of Islay. The skipper, Derek Reader, was in his bunk below, possibly sleeping off the effects of his celebrating. He had left the bosun, John Pirie, at the wheel, with instructions to wake him up before entering the Sound of Islay. Pirie failed to do so; in fact he later admitted to the enquiry that he had had a lot to drink and was steering the vessel whilst 'in a stupor'. The enquiry found the skipper at fault for being below at an inappropriate time and his certificate was suspended.

What actually happened is that the two trawlers entered the Sound of Islay at full speed in the dark. *Wyre Defence* was pulling slightly ahead – perhaps there was a bit of a race going on between them. Anyway, *Wyre Majestic* left it too late to adjust course to negotiate the kink in the Sound, which is a notoriously difficult piece of water at the best of times; narrow and troubled by surging tidal races.

Wyre Majestic hit the rocks at full speed and with an eight knot tide running from astern. Grounding at about 18 knots therefore, tore open the bottom of the boat at the engine room and ruptured her fuel tank. It must have made a really horrible, sickening noise.

It is hard to know who to feel more sympathy for; maybe the skipper down below, wrenched from the soft folds of sleep into a world of grinding metal, listing decks and thumping heads, powerless to do anything much, apart from loudly cursing Pirie and his future descendants for countless generations. On the other hand, anyone who has ever tried to steer a

74

boat, will have some sympathy for Pirie, struggling to get the *Wyre Majestic* to respond to his (admittedly late) attempts to turn it away from those horrible black rocks and the looming shore. We've all had 'Oh-Shit! Look what I've done' moments, though hopefully, few as spectacular as that one.

Wyre Defence returned to the scene and the Port Askaig lifeboat was quickly alongside. Both of these vessels attempted to pull *Majestic* off the rocks but without success.

Eventually the lifeboat took five of the crew ashore and Derek Reader, along with the mate, Phil Huff and engineer, Charlie Timmins, remained on board the stricken trawler for 10 days, hoping that a big tide would allow tugs to pull her free. *Majestic* however, had settled too heavily on the rocks and had to be given up. Though a lot of whisky has matured at Bunnhabhain since 1974, there she still sits, looking more pathetic than majestic these days.

The Chequered Career of the *Wyre Majestic*

Wyre Majestic appears to have been built by Cochranes at Selby in the mid 1950s and had a brief but interesting career. In February 1958 she ran into cliffs below the lighthouse on the Mull of Galloway. Then, less than two years later, she ran aground in almost the very same place. In neither incident were any lives lost.

In January 1964 she returned to port with a dent in her bows after colliding with an iceberg off the North Cape of Iceland. That incident happened at night after an

Arctic gale blew up without warning. The skipper at that time was Alec Middleton, who seems to have been able to deal quickly and effectively with a very frightening situation. Ordering an immediate 'stop engines' he managed within half an hour to steer *Majestic* out of harms way, while at the same time using the radio telephone to warn several other trawlers which were following behind. These all managed to avoid the white ice menace, apart from the *Irvana*, which damaged her propeller and eventually had to be towed to safety by another trawler. Middleton was considered to be a bit of a hero for his cool response in that time of sudden crisis.

Other Fishy Fleetwood Failures

A number of Fleetwood trawlers have experienced problems around the Islay coast over the years.

Anida

The trawler *Anida* apparently ran aground on Frenchman's Rocks, near Portnahaven on 28 October 1924. Nine men were lost.

Cormoran

On 18 January, 1926 the Fleetwood trawler *Cormoran* ran aground on rocks near Kilchiaran Bay. Five of the crew managed to get ashore and were looked after by locals; another five were thrown into the sea and managed to climb into the lifeboat. Unfortunately the lifeboat was leaking, had no sails or rowlocks and they were without shelter or dry clothing. They finally washed up on Tiree three days later, suffering from frostbite, starving and completely exhausted. It is quite a way to Tiree from Islay but it could have been worse – the next landfall would have been America! The skipper stayed with the stricken trawler and was unfortunately killed when the boiler exploded.

Ida Adams

On the 21 November 1930, in poor weather and fog, the trawler *Ida Adams* also ran aground on the Frenchman's Rocks. Despite having to deal with a galley fire and the rapid demise of the vessel, the crew of 12 and the skipper's dog were able to abandon ship and get ashore in their small rowing boat.

Criscilla

The trawler *Criscilla* was only two years old when she was sailing south through the Sound of Islay on the 2 November 1931, laden down with 2,500 stone of fish. The weather was misty and the crew were watching out for the McArthur's Head lighthouse and the light on Black Rocks, almost opposite. Unfortunately the light on Black Rocks was not working and they ran aground. Serious efforts were made to salvage the vessel, including one of the earliest attempts to raise a ship using compressed air. This was almost successful, but as she lifted with the air, *Criscilla* snagged on another rock by the stern, turned over and sank. There she lies still, in the close company of two other anonymous vessels which have come to grief at the same spot.

San Sebastian and Luneda

The early months of 1937 were particularly bad for the Fleetwood trawlers. On 16 January, the *San Sebastian* hit rocks two miles offshore near Ardbeg. The ship went down quickly and four of the crew were lost. The other nine managed to cling to rocks. DCL's puffer *Pibroch*, on her way to Lagavulin, managed to pick up eight of them. The skipper, who had been washed onto a further rock, was missed and eventually had to swim for the shore. He was spotted by a local fisherman called McAllister, who got his boat out and rescued the exhausted captain.

On the 9 February, less than a month later, Fleetwood's *Luneda* ran aground in almost exactly the same spot. This time it was in snowy conditions; the crew managed to get into their boat but were afraid to head for the shore because of all the reefs and rocks. Once again they were rescued by the *Pibroch*, trying to get on with its whisky business. This made a total of 22 Fleetwood fishermen rescued by the *Pibroch* in the space of less than four weeks. This vessel now acquired the nickname of 'the Fleetwood lifeboat' and apparently its crew were frequently presented with boxes of fish by grateful, appreciative Fleetwood trawlermen over the following months.

Exmouth

It was on the 9 of March, 1938, in a spooky coincidence that the Fleetwood trawler *Exmouth* was wrecked on Smaull Point, practically yards from the place where the *Exmouth of Newcastle* had come to grief so tragically in 1847. Such was the swell that three of the crew were washed away and drowned when they were trying to get into the ship's boat. The other eight managed to survive.

Wyre Defence

In 1974, only a month after she saw her sister ship *Wyre Majestic* founder on the rocks in the Sound of Islay, *Wyre Defence* did the same thing. Less than one kilometre south of Port Askaig there is a small lighthouse, just below Dunlossit House. There, one late autumn night, *Wyre Defence*, by some almost unbelievable coincidence, grounded herself. The crew and the skipper must have thought that narrow piece of water was jinxed. However, extremely fortunately for the crew, she managed to refloat and the incident became an almost private matter, not brought to the public's gaze.

Whisky on the rocks – again

Wyre Majestic may not have been the only vessel lured onto rocks by the distraction of a distillery. I heard an interesting story from coastguard Harold Hastie about a Swiss couple, Alain and Kate Chappex. They had been admiring the view of Ardbeg distillery from their yacht the *Maryland*, perhaps too attentively, when they hit a submerged reef. The collision resulted in severe damage to the propeller and rudder and caused a minor leak.

Harold helped tow them to Port Ellen though eventually the boat had to go to Crinan for repairs. Mr and Mrs Chappex came back to Islay during the whisky festival and had such a good time in the Bruichladdich warehouse with Duncan McGillvray that they said they were glad in a way that the accident had happened because they had met such nice people, discovered the joys of single malt. They are now regular visitors and are very keen to buy a house on the island.

THE YELLOW SUBMARINE

On 27 May 2005, John Baker, a fisherman from Port Ellen, was out in his boat *Harvester* about three miles south-west of the Mull of Oa. He was looking for creel buoys when he saw something that looked highly unusual; floating on the sea was a **yellow submarine**. It was sitting upright, just below the surface, about 10 feet long, with wires, perhaps the remains of an umbilical, trailing out from behind it. The submarine was the brightest canary yellow, seemed to be a very hi-tech piece of kit and had MOD markings and a serial number on it. As he considered the **sunflower submersible** not only lost, but a hazard to shipping, John attached a line to it and towed it behind *Harvester* back to Port Ellen.

He contacted his brother-in-law Harold Hastie, who is himself a member of the local Coastguard. They got the **gamboge gondola** ashore thanks to the lifting gear on Harold's boat *Clansman* and then loaded it onto a pick-up truck and drove it to Harold's house where it was stowed in the garden. An impromptu **yellow submarine** party ensued, with lots of whisky consumed (any excuse will do on Islay) much singing and parodying of the relevant Beatles song and trophy photographs of the rescued **saffron sub** taken.

The Navy were contacted but initially denied that they had lost this particular **xanthic bathyscaphe**, or indeed that such a **floating lemon** existed. The *Ileach* got hold of some photos of the **fulvous vessel** and before long the item was out on the world-wide media. The Navy, far from being engaged in an all out hunt for **ochre October**, were instead very slow to admit that the **jaundiced Nautilus** was theirs; it turns out it is a Remotely Operated Vehicle (ROV) which is used to drop depth charges onto unexploded World War II ordinance whenever such dangers are discovered. It was lost from HMS *Penzance* and this may not have been the first time as a similar **primrose propellor** washed up on a Swedish beach about a year before. The **topaz torpedo** was indeed carrying a depth charge underneath at the time John Baker found it, though fortunately it was unarmed. This little **crocus coracle** is worth between half and three-quarters of a million pounds.

It took three months for the Navy to reclaim the **canary craft**. It was at dawn on 8 September that HMS *Blyth*, a Navy minesweeper, quietly glided into Port Ellen harbour on a surreptitious retrieval mission. Naturally, the local communication channels were quickly active and by the time the **cadmium canister** was brought back to the quay-side, a number of people had gathered. Mark Reynier was also there, to present the Commander of HMS *Blyth* with half a case of Bruichladdich Yellow Submarine — WMD II single malt. The Commander was slightly embarrassed by the whole situation, especially as more photographs were taken, but nonetheless he accepted the whisky. The other half of the case went to Harold Hastie and John Baker.

It is not possible to claim Navy vessels as salvage but John waits patiently to see if he will be thanked by the Navy for retrieving this **citric Seawolf** and returning it to its owners.

WEAPONS OF MASS DESTRUCTION

After the evil attacks on the twin towers of 9 September 2001, there was a great swell of sympathy around the world for the USA. It would have been no surprise to anyone that their government machinery swung quickly into action creating whole departments whose aim was to identify terrorists in every corner of the globe who were plotting more imaginative evil ways to bring death and destruction to the innocent citizens of the Western democracies.

It did come as a bit of a surprise however, when we learned, in 2003, that the Defence Threat Reduction Agency in Fort Belvoir, Virginia, were focussing their clandestine attentions on a nest of fanatical extremists concocting chemical weapons to be unleashed on an unsuspecting world – where? – Bruichladdich Distillery, on the Rinns of Islay.

Chemical weapons along with biological, nuclear, radiological and high explosives, are the specific concerns of the DTRA. The most sophisticated chemical weapons are devastating and indiscriminate – you simply uncork the bottle, the evil genie comes out – and abracadabra! – we all fall down. When you put it like that, it is quite understandable that Ursula Stearns of the DTRA should be spying on Bruichladdich distillery through the webcams.

When her cover was blown and her attentions skilfully deflected by counter-insurgency agent, Mark Reynier, she replied,

I apologize for the delay in responding to you especially since you replied so quickly to my question. I appreciate the information you provided.

The use of the webcam is purely personal. I saw a television program about your dis-

tillery and have enjoyed watching your webcams ever since.

I work at the Defense Threat Reduction Agency. Our mission is to safeguard the US and its allies from weapons of mass destruction (chemical, biological, radiological, nuclear and high explosives). Our area deals with the implementation of the Chemical Weapons Convention so we go to sites to

verify treaty compliance. I still find it very funny that their chemical processes look very similar to your distilling process. I mean no disrespect. As part of a training class we went to a brewery for familiarization with reactors, batch processors, evaporators, etc. before going in the field. It just goes to show how 'tweaks' to the process flow, equipment, etc., can create something very pleasant (whiskey) or deadly (chemical weapons).

When I look at your webcams, I think about my time spent in that area of the world and thoughts of going back. If I do, your island and your distillery are on my list of places to visit.

I hope you've had a good summer. Thanks again.

Ursula Stearns
Defense Threat Reduction Agency
Operations Support Division/Security
Countermeasures Branch
8725 John J. Kingman Road
Fort Belvoir, VA

I checked the internet myself in a sneaky piece of counter-insurgency and found that Ursula Stearns, of Sterling, Virginia, is a keen (though not very effective) participant in fun runs and turkey trots throughout the state of Virginia. If Mark Reynier wants to lure her someday to Bruichladdich, in order to take her into custody and torture the truth from her, all he has to do is to up-grade the Bruichladdich 10k run to a turkey trot (whatever that is) and she may be unable to resist the temptation to compete. Once she is gobbled up by the Bruichladdich Al Qaeda nest, they can get back to plotting the overthrow of the civilized world.

In the meantime, I had to resort to a piece of musical satire, as a way of declaring support for the misunderstood freedom fighters of Bruichladdich (I wonder what 'the dog's bollocks' is in Arabic?). My first effort was considered too sensitive in its attack on Uncle Sam, so Mark pleaded with me to change the last two lines. With a flourish of foolish bravado, I give the original version here, and prepare to deal with attacks by agents of both the USA and Al Qaeda — I wonder who will be the first to reach me?

WE CAN'T LET AL QAEDA GET THEIR HANDS ON THIS

There's a secret installation on the western seas
Cunningly disguised among the Hebrides
It might seem innocent to those who are naive
But this could bring a super power to its knees.

CHORUS

So be careful how you're steppin'
Round this deadly lethal weapon
And tell all the patriots it's time to enlist
We've got to take some action
'Gainst this weapon of mass distraction
Oh we can't let Al Qaeda get their hands on this.

Now I am a US Internet spy
And I've seen what they're up to with my own eyes
They say it's only whisky but I'm tellin' you,
They tested it on the local folk and I've seen what it can do.

CHORUS

So be careful how you're steppin'
Round this deadly lethal weapon
And tell all the patriots it's time to enlist
We've got to take some action
'Gainst this weapon of mass distraction
Oh we can't let Al Qaeda get their hands on this.

The scary thing is it's made from a kind of
  grass
With biological action to give it critical mass
And if they get it up to 90 ABV
It's going to be an awesome WMD

CHORUS

So be careful how you're steppin'
Round this deadly lethal weapon
And tell all the patriots it's time to enlist
We've got to take some action
'Gainst this weapon of mass distraction
Oh we can't let Al Qaeda get their hands on this.

So I got me a sample and sent it to the lab
The lab report came back sayin' 'Man this
  stuff's not bad!'
So I am defecting 'cos one thing's clear
I'd rather die from this stuff than from
  American beer

CHORUS

So be careful how you're steppin'
Round this deadly lethal weapon
And tell all the patriots it's time to enlist
We've got to take some action
'Gainst this weapon of mass distraction
Oh we can't let Al Qaeda get their hands on this.
Oh we can't let Al Qaeda get their hands on this.
Oh we can't let Al Qaeda get their hands on this.

This song is available on my third whisky album, *One for the Road* (CDTRAX313) or as a download from Bruichladdich's website.

SECTION THREE

WHISKY BEASTS

AIRIGH NAM BEIST

If you ever walk up the hill from Ardbeg distillery to find the water source (never under-estimate the importance of water for making whisky!) you will find some interesting, spooky spots. The main loch from which Ardbeg's water flows is called Loch Uigeadail, which apparently means 'dark and mysterious place'. It has now given its name to a dark and mysterious spirit, which at 52.4% abv, was described by Michael Jackson as 'a shock to the system'. We do not know why the Loch has this 'dark and mysterious' reputation.

Lower down the hill is a place called Solam, which is the location of a plague or fever village. The story attached to the now-vanished village of Solam is that once upon a time, a sailor came here carrying the plague, which soon started to spread through the local inhabitants. Solam was declared a quarantine settlement, isolated from the rest of the community and if anyone else started to show plague symptoms, they were sent there to embrace their fate. The 'healthy' members of the community left provisions for the infected victims on a stone, but there was no direct contact. Presumably, when the food was no longer collected, the last plague sufferer had died. If you know where to look, there are faces carved on some stones around here. The carvings are supposed to have been done by a lonely shepherd with time on his hands, but some say they were left by inhabitants of the fever village trying to distract themselves from the horrible fate awaiting them.

Despite all this legend potential, it is a place near the distillery called Airigh nam Beist that has given us a spine-chilling tale. The meaning of the place-name could be 'shelter of the beast' or more prosaically 'place of the cattle'. Of course it has a lovely resonance to English speakers because it sounds vaguely like Hairy Beast. There follows the gist of this 'unworldly tale' as relayed in a booklet to members of the Ardbeg Committee.

A burn runs from a lochan near Airigh nam Beist to Ardbeg distillery and some years ago, there came a day when the supply of water began to slow. By dusk it had become the merest trickle – certainly not enough for the requirements of the distillery. Three of the distillery night-shift set off, carrying lanterns against the dark, to investigate the problem. They had little choice of course, but each of them, inwardly remembering ghost stories and tales about this 'spooky' part of the hill, would rather not be venturing out at all. Indeed, it was probably this unspoken trepidation that resulted in three of them going on an errand that one man could probably have managed fine on his own.

Naturally, the wind was howling and rain began to fall as the last trace of light leaked out of the western sky. Approaching Airigh nam Beist, night shift workers Johnston, McPhail and Brown suddenly heard a fearsome sound that stopped them dead in their tracks and sent their blood racing. It was strange and eldritch kind of howl – not human, but hard to identify as any known animal. They stood a moment, trying to make sense of it when the sound came again, but slightly differently – this time it had a deep-throated bleat to it – though still quite unearthly. Johnston whispered a question; could it be a ram, or a deer, perhaps, caught in a fence and howling for its life? McPhail didn't think so. Brown kept his council.

The sound had come from behind a small hill in the direction in which they were headed, so despite inner fears and strong desires to get out of there, they all felt they had to proceed and take what comfort they could in being in company. However, instead of proceeding in single file as before, there was now an unspoken agreement that they should proceed shoulder to shoulder. They crested the hillock like that, their lanterns swinging and creaking in the wind and hardly penetrating the darkness that seemed to thicken all around them.

They saw something move. The cry came up at them again, but this time it seemed to have a more piteous and pathetic quality. They thought they were looking at something resembling the head of a ram with curved horns. It was hard to discern shadows from substance. Brown said, 'It seems like it's stuck in the wet peat at the edge of the lochan. We'd better try to help it out.' The others agreed, though with little enthusiasm.

Setting down their lanterns, the three men tried to lay hands on the creature, which twisted and growled. 'It's a big bugger!' said McPhail, as he tried to maintain his footing in the slippery muck. Above the gurgling of the burn outflow and the growling of the creature, they could hear definite sucking sounds as their efforts were slowly rewarded. However, as the creature began to emerge from the bog, the men became disorientated. Firstly, they were aware of an evil stench suddenly assailing their nostrils; a visceral smell, more hideous than any animal or human waste, more gut-wrenching than decaying flesh. Instinctively, the men let go and staggered back, clutching their throats, choking and gagging.

By this stage, however, the creature was sufficiently free from the mire, that it was able, with jerks and straining convulsions, to free itself. As it did so, no ram emerged from the black mud, but an enormous, diabolical creature, more than eight feet high. It stood, stooping unsteadily on two legs, its juddering head crowned with curved horns, its eyes red and glaring in the dark, and its anguished, evil-looking mouth, full of black and broken fangs, emitting a blood-curdling, deafening roar.

Its body seemed encased in neither skin nor hide, but some odd mixture of fur and scale and bare bone. It roared again, shaking all over and pulled itself to its full height staring with raw hatred and terrible intent at the three men. Brown was already trying to flee the spot and Johnston at least had the sense to avert his gaze, but McPhail found his eyes glued to the creature's malevolent stare.

He said afterward that he had never experienced anything like it in his life –

the feeling was like a migraine so severe that you could smell burning and a sharp blade slicing through your innards at the same time. Suddenly, and just as the men expected to die horrible deaths, the beast turned and fled into the dark in the direction of the hill and mysterious Loch Uigeadail, leaving behind only the remaining stench and the leaden lumps of fear in the distillery workers' hearts.

They needed no encouragement to return to Ardbeg by the quickest route possible, and once safely inside the warm, lit distillery, they headed for the emergency bottle of medicinal Ardbeg. Hands shaking, they filled glasses and drank wordlessly, the first mouthfuls going down like water in the throat of a man dying of thirst. Obviously, they told their tale to others, for that is how it has come to be handed down. Not everyone believed the story, for distillery workers have a certain reputation for seeing things that don't really exist, especially on the night shift. But anyone who knew these men personally could not doubt that the experience had changed them in some fundamental way. They became more serious and more withdrawn; indeed, within two months, McPhail was dead of a mysterious illness.

The local people are now even more wary of that stretch of hillside and it has an abandoned, unfrequented feel about it. Ardbeg recently released a dram under the name of Airigh nam Beist — locals call it 'the wee beastie' — a double is known as 'a big beastie'. Some folk have been known to cross themselves with the protecting spirit before knocking it back to provide a bit of internal courage, whenever that might be called for, especially if it's a wee *deoch an dorus*, before heading home in the dark after a *ceilidh*.

LOATHLY WORMS

The informal club of distillery managers on Islay is called The Condenser Club because, just as Ireland has no snakes, Islay has no worms – all the distilleries have condensers rather than worm tubs for cooling. It might be true that there are no worm tubs in any of the distilleries but other worms have been known to pop up from time to time.

The Minister's Worm

Master storyteller David Campbell (I wonder if he is related to storiologist John Francis Campbell?) once told me a worm story when we were in New York together. Apparently one of the ministers on Islay was becoming concerned about the amount of whisky being consumed by people in his parish. (It may have been the Reverend Archibald Robertson, who complained in the Statistical Account of Islay 1791–99, 'This island hath a liberty of brewing whisky, without being under the necessity of paying the usual excise duty to government. We have not an excise officer on the whole island.')

Whoever it was, he decided he had to make a point to the congregation and so he appeared before them one Sunday flashing a particularly stern gaze from his pulpit. Without saying anything, but with glowering looks, he produced two glasses, one filled with water and one with whisky, which he placed upon the pulpit shelf. Then casting around further stares full of disapproval and disgust, he produced a large worm from a tin that had been concealed under his cloak. He held it up for the congregation to see it wriggle and squirm then he dropped it into the glass of water. After a few seconds, he fished it out,

gave it a shake, the water droplets reaching the front pews but his theatrical scowl reaching right to the back of the church.

Next, he dropped it into the glass of whisky, where it wriggled for a few seconds even more animatedly than before but then stopped altogether. A shadow of triumph joined the disdain of his beetled brows for a moment as he once again fished out the worm and held it up, limp and dead for the congregation to see. Finally he spoke, his voice harsh with contempt, 'Here we have one of the lowliest of God's creatures; did you see how it was happy and healthy and thriving in the pure, clean water from the hill? But after only moments in the Devil's Brew, the filthy *uisge beatha*, look what happened to it! What does that tell you?' he demanded, his voice rising to a crescendo of derision.

Just then, old MacPhee, at the back of the church, called out in answer, 'If you drink enough whisky – you'll never be troubled by worms!'

The Worm of Jura

This is taken straight from Thomas Pennant's book of 1772 *A Tour of Scotland and Voyage to the Hebrides*;

> I had some account here of a worm, that in a less pernicious degree, bears some resem-

blance to the Furia internalis of Linnaeus, which in the vast bogs of Kemi drops on the inhabitants, eats into the flesh and occasions a most excruciating death. The fillan, a little worm of Jura, small as a thread and not an inch in length, like the furia, insinuates itself under the skin, causes a redness and great pain, flies swiftly from part to part, but is curable by a poultice of cheese and honey.

What – not whisky?

The Loathly Worm

In *The Gaelic Underworld*, edited by Ronald Black, there is a section on serpents and one of those was the big beast of Scantcastle (present day Scanistle, which lies between Ballygrant and Port Askaig). According to the entry;

> This serpent devoured seven horses on its way to Loch-in-Daal. A ship was lying at anchor in the loch at the time, and a line of barrels filled with deadly spikes, and with pieces of flesh laid upon them, was placed from the shore to the ship. Tempted by the flesh, the 'loathly worm' made its way out on the barrels and was killed by the spikes and cannon.

Peggy Earl had a version of this story in which the serpent (a dragon this time) was killed by the famous Godred Crovan. This is Godred White Hand, not to be confused with his grandson Godred the Black. Indeed Godred Crovan was himself the son of Harald the Black so the whole family may have been colour-coded. This would not have been much use to one of White Hand's sons, for he was Harald the Blind, or at least that was his name after he had his eyes put out by his older brother Lagman the Bad-tempered. It was Crovan's third son, Olaf the Dwarf, who inherited the Kingdom of Dublin, Man and the Sudreys; he was good at keeping a low profile. Godred Crovan died in 1095 of the pestilence, probably worm-induced, and is buried at Carragh Bhan, near Kintra.

Anyway, according to Peggy Earl, Godred Crovan arrived on his galley into Loch Indaal and heard the terrible story of how the loathly worm had just about eaten everything and everyone on the island. He lured the serpent to the shores of the loch by calling it names and leaving a trail of horses, one after the other, along the road. The dragon could not resist eating all the horses, so by the time it reached the loch, it was rather full and sluggish and probably suffering from galloping indigestion. Godred strung the barrels, bristling with spikes in a row towards the ship and waving another tasty morsel in front of the 'worm' fled nimbly across the barrels. The dragon pursued him but was so full and fat that it ripped its belly open on the spikes and Godred was able to finish it off with cannon or his knife, or whatever.

It is truly amazing what you can do with some old whisky barrels.

Cladville Cakes

According to a poem by Swedish writer Lennart Hellsing, the famous whisky cakes of the Rinns were made to a recipe once kept secret by dragons and snakes; I think I tried some once in the House of Bliss.

These are the good old Cladville Cakes
That mother Marti daily bakes —
Toasted by a thunderbolt
Dipped in whisky lakes
Lovely, delightful Cladville Cakes!

Delicious, delectable Cladville Cakes
Of yore a secret of dragons and snakes;
Disclosed was the recipe
By some odd mistakes —
Now everyone makes these good old cakes!

OF MONSTERS AND MOUNTAINSIDE DRAMS

One of Islay's most inventive sons, Donald MacDonald, is not widely recognised for his great achievements and the islanders have almost all forgotten that he existed. Donald was a Victorian engineer (born in 1824) who worked at the cutting edge of some of the most interesting technologies of his day. His two lifelong interests were railways and the rapidly developing technology of underwater exploration.

In terms of railway engineering Donald's specialism was tunnelling. He worked as an apprentice on Brunel's Thames Tunnel project (1841), the first underwater tunnel. He was a great advocate of using tunnelling to take railways through mountainous terrain and seriously fell out with the Scottish railway builders because they ignored his advice. The Kyle of Lochalsh Line (1860s) and the West Highland Line (1880s) were both designed to avoid tunnels, choosing a contouring design instead. This made them beautifully scenic railways but ones which involve long journeys. A design based on tunnelling routes, following the Roman principle of the straight line being the shortest distance between two points would have achieved shorter, faster journeys which incidentally would have been more energy efficient.

Partly out of huff and partly because of his other interests MacDonald worked on an entirely different scheme which was one of the engineering feats of the 19th century. Underwater exploration was developing a pace at that time, the first underwater air regulator was developed in 1865, allowing divers to move around relatively freely on the sea bed. Jules Verne's book *Twenty Thousand Leagues Under the Sea* (1870) fired the imagination of scientists and inventors all over the world and MacDonald was a huge enthusiast. Combining his expertise in tunnelling with that of underwater technology, MacDonald was commissioned by the government to carry out an audacious but secret tunnelling project.

Over a number of years, Donald MacDonald supervised a project which linked the southern end of Loch Ness by a long tunnel to the eastern end of Loch Morar. This allowed the stranded monsters who inhabited the two lochs to meet each other and thus ensured that the breed should never die out. These creatures, which are related to the plesiosaurs, had survived in the deep lochs of Scotland for more than 70 million years but with increasing pressure of traffic and tourism, the shy creatures, especially the one(s) in Loch Ness were beginning to feel very uncomfortable.

As a final touch of genius, MacDonald also managed later to build an underground tunnel from the western end of Loch Morar to the sea. This is a distance of less than two miles on the map but he chose to build the tunnel at a much deeper level to ensure that the creatures, when exiting the loch should not come up in the shallow sea, frightening swimmers and beachcombers.

MacDonald, having studied the plesiosaurs closely, intuited that they were probably migratory creatures very similar to the

91

Atlantic salmon, on which they would have naturally fed. So after MacDonald's tunnel was built, Morag and Nessie (a bit of a misnomer; Nessie, the larger of the two, was in fact the male) could roam the farthest oceans in search of tasty fish and with all the freedom and space they could want but still come back to the freshwater lochs to spawn. This is the reason why sightings of the 'monsters' became less frequent after the beginning of the 20th century despite many nosy people trying to spy on them.

MacDonald, in his leisure time was a keen mountaineer and being an Islayman he was also a whisky lover. He loved nothing more than roaming the mountains of Scotland in his kilt and hiking boots with a hip flask of finest Islay malt in his sporran (this is not a contra-

diction in terms; anyone who has climbed mountains in a kilt knows that the sporran, especially when loaded with whisky, is best worn on the side or hip, to avoid serious bruising of sensitive body parts).

Donald's love of mountains and his enthusiasm for railways and tunnels led him naturally to Switzerland. In that country the mountains are enormous, the trains always run on time and Swiss engineers are so fond of tunnels that they sometimes build them from one valley to another for no reason at all; the Swiss Alpine landscape, if you could x-ray it, is actually very similar to a Swiss cheese.

So it was that Donald came to be setting off up the Jungfrau from Interlaken on a sunny day in June in the year 1874. On the way up, he met two local men, Herr Hofweber, who owned and managed the local brewery, and his son. After some pleasant conversation walking up the track together, the Hofwebers insisted on treating their new friend to a sample of their art at a wayside inn. Donald was so refreshed and impressed with his cool glass of Rugenbräu beer that he produced his hipflask and poured the Hofwebers a dram of Islay malt each. He was not at all bothered that they both put an ice cube in their whisky, in fact, as it was such a hot day, he did the same with his.

His Swiss companions were absolutely blown away with the quality of the spirit Donald poured them and demanded to know what it was; all they could compare it with was kirsch, schnapps or French brandy none of which came anywhere close. When Donald told them that malt whisky, at its simplest, was a distillation of beer, the father and son Hofweber looked at each other in amazement and a secret family ambition was born – to someday turn their beer into nectar like this.

That family ambition took 130 years to realise, but eventually, Bruno Hofweber, a descendent of the men who met Donald on the mountain in 1874, has now managed to turn the Rugenbräu beer into whisky. To help him in this quest, he contacted Jim McEwan, master distiller on Islay, and asked for his advice. Jim, one of the few Ileachs aware of the story of Donald MacDonald was only too happy to help.

The Hofwebers now make a Swiss Highland single malt whisky which is matured in beautiful oloroso sherry butts inside a whisky cellar at the Rugenbräu brewery. I was privileged to be present when that cellar was opened at 12 minutes past 12 o'clock on 12 December 2008 by Bruno Hofweber and his special guest, Jim McEwan. Jim unveiled a mural depicting the kilted Donald MacDonald in the company of two Victorian Swiss gentlemen with the Jungfrau behind.

In a fitting tribute to the day when the dream was born, Bruno Hofweber has pledged to mature some of his whisky each year in an ice cave on the 'Top of Europe', at the Jungfaujoch, which is 3,454 metres above sea level. This Ice Label whisky recalls the day in 1874 when Donald MacDonald and two members of the Hofweber family forged a lasting link between Scotland and Switzerland by drinking whisky on the rocks halfway up the Jungfrau. I have tasted this natural strength Ice Label whisky and consider it to be far and away the best whisky made in Switzerland at the present time.

SMOKEY THE CAT

I met Smokey the cat the very first time I visited Bowmore distillery. Christine Logan told me how Smokey had just sort of appeared one day and casually took up residence at the distillery with that cat-like air of ownership and belonging. She was an attractive cat, very popular with visitors, who loved to take photographs of her. When I spoke to Eddie McAffer (distillery manager) recently, he told me that after Smokey died she was never replaced and that when he goes down at night with a torch to pull samples he sometimes has the distinct impression that the cat is there around his feet. His hair goes up on end and he is convinced that the spirit of Smokey lives on. Hopefully her spirit will live on in my poem at least.

SMOKEY THE CAT

They say cats have more than one life
With re-incarnation and that.
Whether it's true
All that cat deja vu,
Smokey's a born again cat.

There's something about her that takes you
Back to the Lords of the Isles
When the cats of Finlaggan
Would go scallywaggin'
For miles and miles and miles.

Smokey the cat came from nowhere;
Just wisped in under some door;
Sniffed quietly around
And knew that she'd found
The best place to stay in Bowmore.

It's the way she melts into the shadows
Or suddenly creeps up on folk
She'll always find you
Slinking behind you
The cat who was named after smoke.

She'd arrived at Bowmore distillery
Where the finest malt whisky is made.
There was no welcome mat
For Smokey the cat
But she liked the place — so she stayed.

She sits on the sill of the maltings
On days when the weather is nice
And while one eye sleeps
The other one keeps
A lookout for small birds and mice.

Small birds and mice eat the barley
So Smokey confronts them foursquare
But she pulls in her claws
And quietly ignores
The Angels who come for their share.

Felines don't care for whisky
Everyone understands that
But that peaty odour
Beneath the pagoda
Owes something to Smokey the cat.

On Islay people made whisky
Long before it was chic.
The cat from Bowmore
Is nothing more
Than the ghost of the island's peat-reek.

THE WHITE HORSE

The following tale is found in John Francis Campbell's *Tales of the West Highlands.* Campbell says 'the story was collected about 150 years ago from an old man of 80 called Hugh mac-in-deor. He in turn got it from a man called Aonghas Gruama (frowning Angus) who was himself the subject of many queer tales.'

The story of the widow and her three daughters is an international folk tale and many variations on it are found in Scotland. Sometimes the horse is black or grey, or other details are also different. It is no surprise that the Islay version has a wee injection of whisky into it. Italo Calvino has a version of this in his book Italian Folktales, called *The Three Chicory Gatherers.* In that version, instead of a horse there is a dragon which the third sister outwits by getting him drunk

The Widow and her Three Daughters

There was once a widow who had three daughters. They had very little money — only what they earned from spinning and a kailyard for growing food.

A white horse started coming to the garden and eating the kail. The eldest daughter went out to shoo the beast away. She took the distaff from her spinning wheel and she slapped the horse on its rump but the distaff stuck to the horse and to her hand. The horse galloped off and she was dragged along until they came to a castle.

On entering the castle the horse turned into a man who told her he was the son of the King. She was very well looked after and next morning he said he had to go hunting with his father but that when he returned they should have dinner and make plans

for their wedding. He gave her the keys to the castle and told her she could have the freedom of the place — but he pointed out one room that she was not to enter under any circumstances.

After he left she started looking into all the castle rooms. Every one seemed finer and grander that the last one. When she came at last to the forbidden room she hesitated but her curiosity was great and she thought what harm could there be in just having a wee peek.

She opened the door and started to step inside but suddenly gasped in horror — the room was full of dead women and there was blood everywhere. Her foot, which had entered the room, was now red up to the ankle. She quickly closed the door, locked it and tried to clean her foot but the blood would not come off!

Just then a little grey cat came by and asked her for a drop of milk. 'Shoo! You stupid beast.' she said, 'How can I take care of you when I am in such a predicament?'

When the King's son came home he asked her if she had been a good woman while he was gone. 'Oh yes,' she said, but he demanded to see her feet. When he saw the blood he quickly drew his sword and chopped off her head.

The next day the white horse was back at the kailyard and this time the middle sister went out with her distaff and whacked the horse. Again the distaff stuck to the horse and she was dragged off to the castle. Exactly the same thing happened, except that when she opened the forbidden door it was even worse because her own sister was inside, head severed from the body. She slammed the door on the awful scene and gasped for breath. Just like the first sister she spurned the little grey cat and eventually suffered the same fate at the hands of the King's son.

The day after that, the white horse was back and this time the youngest sister went out and ended up in the castle. Exactly the same events unfolded but the youngest sister being of a kinder disposition fetched some milk for the wee grey cat. The cat drank some of the milk and then began to lick the youngest sister's foot, removing all the blood.

That night, the King's son, delighted to have found a trustworthy woman at last, made plans for the wedding to take place in a few days. The following day when he went hunting again the wee grey cat came round and spoke to the woman saying, 'Even if you wed him you will not last long. Here is what you have to do if you want to live and to see your sisters alive again. Go back into the forbidden room. On a shelf at the back of the room is a bottle of golden liquid. That is the Water of Life. Take some of the liquid and rub it on your sisters' lips.'

Then the little cat gave the youngest daughter other instructions, which she

followed well and this is what happened...

The next three days she spent going round the castle apparently cleaning and sorting out her new home. Each day she chose a large chest and asked him to have it sent back to her mother's cottage in the morning saying that the things inside would be more use to a poor old widow on her own than to a King's son and his new wife.

But each day she revived a sister with the Water of Life and put her in the chest, which was then delivered home by the castle servants. On the third day she hid in the chest herself and took the wee grey cat with her. When the King's son discovered that she had gone he flew into a rage and raced to the widow's cottage. When he rushed in at the door the cat tripped him up and the youngest daughter cut off his head with a sword that had belonged to her father.

The cat persuaded her, however, to rub the Water of Life on the lips of the King's son and as soon as she did so he came back to life, not as the hard-hearted murderer, but as himself — a handsome, refined and charming prince who had been under an evil spell. The grey cat also had a lick of the Water of Life and resumed her form as his beautiful sister, the young princess.

The youngest daughter of the widow and the handsome prince were married and everyone lived happily ever after in the castle, making lots of the fabled Water of Life, under the sign of the white horse.

UNCLE WOLF

Once upon a time, in the neighbourhood of Ballygrant, one of the pupils at the village school was a girl who was spoiled, lazy and greedy. Her parents ran the Change House, and did not have much time to spend with her, so they tried to make up for it by giving her almost anything she wanted.

One day, just before Christmas, the school-teacher said, 'If you are good children and finish writing out all the Gaelic proverbs, I'll give you all some mincemeat pies.' The spoiled girl was hopeless at writing Gaelic and sat for a while making faces, while the other children worked. Then she asked permission to go to the toilet where she sat in a huff eating some toffees she had in her pocket. While sitting there sucking toffees and day-dreaming, she eventually nodded off. When she woke and returned to the class she found that the lesson was finished and so were all the mincemeat pies.

She went home to her mum in tears, complaining loudly that the other children got mince pies and she got none; she was in quite a strop about this perceived injustice. Finally, her mother said, 'Never mind, my dear. If it will cheer you up, I'll bake you a whole tray of mincemeat pies.' The girl's eyes suddenly dried up and began to sparkle with greed instead of tears.

Unfortunately, her mum had no muffin tray to make mince pies in, so she said to her daughter, 'If you want mince pies, I'm afraid you'll have to go to Uncle Wolf's house at Mulreesh and ask nicely to borrow his muffin tray.' The little girl was caught between her greed and her laziness and besides, she was afraid of Uncle Wolf who had a reputation for being bad-tempered. In the end, the thought of a whole tray of mince pies had her salivating all the way along the winding track to Mulreesh.

When, at last, she arrived at Uncle Wolf's house, she knocked on the door. Knock, knock...

'Who's there?'

'It's me.'

'No-one has visited me for months and months. What do you want?'

'Mummy sent me to borrow a muffin tray, so she can make mincemeat pies.'

'Just a minute, till I get my shirt on.' Knock, knock.

'Hold on; wait till I get into my breeks.' Knock, knock.

'For goodness sake, hold your horses! I'm trying to find my boots!'

At last Uncle Wolf opened the door and gave her the muffin tray, but he barked gruffly, 'Tell your mum that I want the tray back tomorrow with a batch of mince pies for me. In fact while she's got the oven on she can make me a bannock too. Oh, and half a mutchkin of whisky to wash it down.' The girl readily agreed and skipped all the way home with the muffin tray. She told her mother about Uncle Wolf's conditions. Her mother then made her a whole tray of mince pies, which she ate at one sitting.

The next day, after much grumbling, she set off once more to Uncle Wolf's house, this time carrying a rather heavy basket containing the tray full of mince pies, a

fresh-baked bannock and a bottle with whisky in it. She had to stop a number of times to rest along the way, and each time she rested she could not resist eating one of the mincemeat pies. By the time she was barely half-way there, the pies were all gone. Soon, her greed and laziness ensured that the bannock was transferred from the basket to her belly, which made it seem somehow easier to carry. Now, however, she was thirsty, cold and tired, so she turned her attention to the bottle of whisky.

She had supped the occasional drop of whisky in the Change House before, when no one was looking, but after polishing off half a mutchkin, she became quite fuzzy-headed and her thinking was even more be-fuddled than usual.

Looking around, she filled the bottle with ditch water, put some deer droppings in the muffin tray and replaced the bannock with an old, dried up cowpat. When Uncle Wolf opened the door, she put the basket down in front of his range and quickly turned to go. 'Bye, Uncle Wolf' she said.

'Just a minute! You wait right here.' said Uncle Wolf, stopping her in her tracks. Uncle Wolf bit into one of the mince pies. 'Yeuch! These taste like shite' he said. Then he bit into the bannock. 'Aargh! It's crap!' Quickly he raised the bottle to his lips to wash away the evil taste, but instead he sprayed a mouthful of ditch water all over the floor. He turned to vent his anger on the girl, but she was already running away down the path towards Ballygrant. Uncle Wolf shouted after her, 'I'll get you for this! Tonight I'm coming to eat you!'

The girl ran all the way home and told her mum, 'Tonight Uncle Wolf is coming to eat me!'

'Don't worry' said her mum, 'I won't let Uncle Wolf harm you.' That night, after the last drinker left the Change House, the girl's mother locked all the doors and windows tightly and went to bed. Unfortunately, she gave no thought to the chimney.

In the middle of the night, the girl woke up to hear Uncle Wolf's voice outside. 'I'm right outside and I'm going to eat you.' Then she heard footsteps on the roof; 'Now I'm on your roof and I'm coming to get you.' The girl covered her ears, but could not help hearing a scuffling noise in the chimney and Uncle Wolf's voice saying 'Now I am in the chimney and I'm coming to eat you.' She hid under the bedclothes, crying,

'Mummy, Mummy, Uncle Wolf is coming!'

Then Uncle Wolf was in the room and his voice was loud and scary.

'I'm right here by your bed and I'm going to eat you now!' The girl curled up in a tight ball, shaking like a leaf and sobbing with fear. Uncle Wolf gave a full-throated growl that built into a howl of excited anticipation. Then he ate the girl all up.

The moral of this story is that spoiled children usually come to a sticky end, especially if they drink someone else's whisky.

WHISKY THE ISLAY GEEP

There are wild goats on Islay — I have seen some; once on the cliffs below the American Monument on the Mull of Oa and another time on a hill above Kilchoman, while waiting with my wife, for the midsummer sunrise with a bottle of Bowmore 17 year old and some chocolate for warmth and energy. They are very imposing creatures (goats I mean, not wives) especially the billy goats with their tall horns and venerable beards.

Billy goats are reputed to have powerful sexual appetites, which may be the reason why the devil, in Scotland, and satyrs elsewhere, are often depicted as having hairy legs and cloven hooves. Somewhere on the Rinns, there is definitely a billy goat that is a randy wee devil, for it managed to impose its carnal attentions on a Cheviot ewe belonging to Andrew Smith of Gearach Farm near Port Charlotte. The resulting offspring is a hybrid — a strange looking animal that is neither sheep nor goat but a mixture of the two. Dr Hugh Reid of the Moredun Foundation examined the photos and said, 'There is no question this is a cross-breed. It has the posture, colourings and markings of a goat but the tucked-in tail of a sheep.'

It is relatively rare for sheep and goats to inter-breed. This is possibly the first case in Scotland. Andrew Smith, the farmer, said, 'I've been lambing for 47 years but I've never seen anything like this.' Apparently, though sheep and goats can mate, they have a chromosome mis-match (sheep have 54 and goats have 60) which means that foetuses do not normally survive, and if they do, they are usually infertile.

There have been various recorded cases of surviving hybrids; in Botswana, a cross resulting from a ram mating with a nanny goat, was christened 'The Toast of Botswana'. It had to be castrated because it was continually mounting both sheep and goats in the enclosure. There are other cases from New Zealand and quite recently from the Rhur area of Germany. A farmer in Australia who put a billy goat amongst the sheep to deter foxes, claimed that dozens of 'lambs' arrived which were half goat half sheep.

There was also once a laboratory experiment that fused goat and sheep embryos. This produced a mosaic of mis-matched sheep and goat parts, some parts woolly and some parts hairy. This was a 'chimera' not a hybrid in the true sense.

The animal born to Mr Smith's ewe was, on the other hand, a true hybrid, or 'blend'. It was entitled therefore 'a geep' and was naturally christened Whisky. My friend Gordon Neil from Carluke read about Whisky the Islay geep in *The Herald* and was inspired to write the song which follows.

Incidentally, in Greek mythology, a Chimera was a fire-breathing monster with the head of a lion, the body of a goat and the tail of a serpent. In Gaelic folklore, there are tales about *glaistigs* (there are some in J. F. Campbell's collection); these are vicious creatures, half woman, half goat, who frequent lonely lochs and rivers. They normally hide their goaty legs under long green dresses and are much dreaded, for although they would sometimes watch over cattle, they are also prone to seducing men with their songs and their beauty; once the men were in their clutches the *glaistig* would suck their blood. I think I'd rather face a Chimera, all things considered.

WHISKY, THE ISLAY GEEP

There's a strange sight in an Islay field,
Coorie doon, all will be revealed,
The secret's out, a'body knows,
It's bizarre as the yeti or a thousand UFO's.

In the field there's a rare wee beast,
Wi' tan legs and a creamy breast,
Its body's broon wi' bits o' black,
A creature standing out from the pack.

Whisky the geep
Half goat and half sheep
An evolutionary leap
Whisky, the Islay geep

The Islay folk, they laugh and mock
At Whisky gamboling with the flock
He's been on the national news
The farmers were warned, 'Lock up yer ewes'

Whisky the geep
His mother must have been asleep
When his daddy made his leap
They made Whisky the Islay geep

CHORUS
Mae mae mae mae
Mae mae mae mae
Mae mae mae mae
Mae mae mae mae

Young Whisky boy is no too braw
Heid like dad, ears like maw
His chromosomes are all mixed up
His mammy thought the billy-goat was a tup

Whisky the geep
Half goat and half sheep
The ewes will get no sleep
Because of whisky the Islay geep

CHORUS
Mae mae mae mae
Mae mae mae mae
Mae mae mae mae
Mae mae mae mae

What a story in all his glory
Whisky the Islay geep
Mae mae mae mae

WHISKY V GEESE

Occasionally, in the peatlands of Islay some evidence of ancient battles is unearthed – a sword, an axe-head, a broken helmet, or even some bones, but otherwise the peatlands seem the quietest place on the island. If you stand there, or walk on the bouncing bog, you do not hear the roar of the ocean or the rush of mountain winds – only the gentle breeze and bird song. Even road traffic can be a faint, far-off hum, similar to the passing of the odd flying insect. This is a solitary, peaceful place where you have the company of wind, clouds, insects and birds, rather than the buzz and laughter of the public house. In some ways the very essence of Islay is in these wetlands. Of course, for whisky lovers, that essence means the phenolic hit of peat-reek, while for bird-watchers it may be the cyclical arrival and departure of flocks of birds.

The peat bogs of Islay were the scene of another battle, much more recently, between factions whose values seemed irreconcilable and incommensurate. This was the famous Battle of the Duich Moss or the Whisky v Geese debacle.

To set the scene – it was back in 1985 and that year the Greenland White-fronted geese would arrive in vast numbers as they did every year, on their way from Greenland to somewhere warmer for the summer, totally oblivious, of course to the battle about to be waged on their behalf.

Islay, and especially the wetlands are a kind of pit-stop for the geese, a place where they can rest and refuel and do whatever geese do together in the squelchy peat. That peat is also, of course, a traditional source of fuel for the islanders and, in a way, a source of flavouring for the island's whisky makers. Scottish Malt Distillers had applied for planning permission to extract peat from the Duich Moss and George Younger, the Secretary of State for Scotland, had weighed the competing interests – extraction (or 'stripping' as it was usually referred to by the other side) against the conservation arguments and the importance of the habitat for the geese. He came down in favour of the whisky makers.

Then Tam Dayell got up in parliament and demanded to know why the Scottish Secretary had contravened the Ramsar convention. Ramsar is a place in Iran, which has given its name to an international protocol for protecting wetlands around the world. Actually, the Islay peatlands were only added to the Ramsar list in 1988, so Tam was exaggerating slightly. The Scottish Secretary explained that he had asked for, and considered all the arguments of the competing factions and made a reasoned decision. He stuck to his guns, though he did say that he would be attaching conditions to the permission to extract peat, in view of the sensitive conservation issues.

Then the scene of the 'whisky v geese' confrontation shifted to Islay. Friends of the Earth, with Jonathon Porritt at the helm, decided to take a Task Force to the Duich Moss to protect the poor defenceless geese from the greedy, selfish predations of those who make strong drink, much like Margaret Thatcher had sailed to the Falklands three years earlier to protect the inhabitants from the evil invading Argentines. Porrit brought with him a rent-a-mob who set about preventing the peat-cutting machinery from being used and he brought a secret weapon, in the shape of the high profile, cute and cuddly David Bellamy, who would surely win over everyone, including distillery employees and hardened drinkers (not necessarily the same people). How could anyone fail to see the justice in protecting an important bird species?

Unfortunately, Friends of the Earth (the very name is unassailable) misjudged the situation completely, as is clearly demonstrated by the title of the leaflet they distributed at the public meeting in Bowmore – 'Whisky or Wildlife'. Anyone who knows Islay would call that a 'no-brainer'. The islanders appreciate the importance of the whisky industry, and most of them enjoy a wee sensation from its product once in a while. On the other hand, there is a definite resentment, especially among farmers, that they have to put up with the ravages of millions of marauding geese, year after year, and cannot do a thing to protect their crops and their livelihood. Of course that resentment has been gently massaged over the years by the introduction of subsidies but back in 1985 it was still an issue. Furthermore, the people of Islay do not take kindly to interfering outsiders telling them what to think and how to do things on their own island.

The public meeting attracted 650 people. It is possible some of them misunderstood the leaflet and thought they were being invited to a free lunch, but it is more likely evidence of the strength of feelings. The Friends of the Earth did not have an easy ride, there was not even a balance of arguments. In fact Porritt and Bellamy were lucky not to be lynched. One local shouted out, 'I will tell you Friends of the Earth, you have picked the wrong time, the wrong place and the wrong people'. The visitors had to beat a hasty retreat and took shelter in the house of a friend and supporter after finding their bags packed and sitting out in the yard when they got back to their hotel. They requested a police escort, which in truth was only reluctantly provided. They thought they were coming as the Task Force but were forced to fly home, like the Argentinians, feathers ruffled, muttering Spanish oaths (or was it Portugeese?).

The postscript to the story is that the European Commision eventually intervened and peat extraction on the Duich Moss was halted, relocating a mile or two to Castlehill. The Duich area was made a Nature Reserve in 1993. So, in the end, a solution was found that met the needs of the whisky companies and the geese defenders – at least for now. Probably something that could have been done without going to war. It's all very well to embark on a crusade, but when you invade an island – watch out.

After his ignominious retreat, David Bellamy said publicly that he would never visit Islay again. One local responded, 'Bloody right he won't! The Greenland

White-fronted Goose enjoys protection but if we see any Green-man Black-affronted Goose-steppers the shotgun is coming out of the cabinet.'

What will happen in the future? Who knows? Perhaps the whisky companies will eventually find a cheap chemical substitute for peat to give smokiness to whisky and climate change will either change the nature of the peatlands themselves or force the Greenland White-fronted goose to switch to the southern hemisphere. I could recommend them a place in Peru.

SECTION FOUR

OTHERWORLD SPIRITS

AN ISLAY GHOST STORY

Everywhere in Scotland has ghosts, usually haunting castles or old houses or else residing in spooky places on the landscape. Many distilleries have ghosts also – often they are old buildings and the ghosts are said to be the spirits of previous workers or owners who died or were killed at the distillery. Islay has its share of ghosts too; here I have chosen some stories that involve places that can be crossing points from one world to another – windows, gateways and bridges.

Window to another World

Many years ago a visitor to the island was spending a holiday as a guest of a well-known distillery, not far from Port Ellen. On the second evening of his stay, after some pleasant conversation and one or two drams, the visitor was making his way to his bedroom with a candle to light the darkness, when he saw a figure ahead of him, near the end of the corridor, walking in the same direction. The passageway was dark with long shadows flickering, but the visitor could see that the person in front of him was not his host, for the host was a tall man and this figure was quite small. Furthermore he seemed to be dressed in fairly antiquated clothing.

When the figure reached the end of the corridor it seemed to melt into thin air or through the wall. The visitor strained his eyes in puzzlement, then he seemed to hear a muffled but distinct thud and immediately a heavy silence descended. Somewhat unnerved by this experience, the visitor made his way to bed.

That night he had a disturbing dream; he found himself being irresistibly drawn towards a window at the end of a passage. The scene was vivid and he seemed to know that the window represented something

dreadful but he could not help himself from being pulled to it. He grasped at furniture and curtains but could not turn or resist the force. Soon he found himself climbing through the window and standing on a high ledge, aware of a sickening gulf stretching below him. He found himself falling – a gut-wrenching sensation and then suddenly the clock struck five and he woke, sitting up and sweating in his bed.

Exactly the same thing happened the following night. In the dream he could feel the night air on his brow as he leaned out over the deep chasm of space. This time however, when he awoke from the dream, he was not in his bed, but out in the corridor, pressing against a blank wall at the end of the passage. Never having walked in his sleep before, he was greatly perturbed by this sequence of events and related the whole thing to his host at breakfast.

The host looked at him seriously and with concern, then he sent for one of the older distillery workers and asked him to join them and tell the visitor a story. The old worker said that about a hundred years ago, before the modern portion of the distillery had been built, a tragic incident happened. Apparently, a man had broken into the distillery, searching for drink; he found whisky in abundance and consumed far too much. Crazed by whisky, he threw himself out of an open window and was killed instantly.

During the rebuild and extension, that window had been blocked up and surrounded by the annexe of new rooms. However, the window would have been at the exact spot where the visitor found himself on waking from his dream. It had been rumoured that the earth-bound spirit of that unfortunate man haunted the distill-ery from time to time; the visitor's experience would seem to suggest that the rumour had some substance.

The Beard Gateway

Way back in history, in a dell on Islay, there was a gate called 'The Beard Gateway'. According to local superstition, in that place unearthly things might be encountered after dark.

One man, travelling home after a session in the pub, was attacked by something foul that he couldn't quite make out. At first it resembled a strange and frightening woman but soon turned into an enormous gaping maw of horrid stench and fearsome sight that tried to devour him completely. Luckily for him he had a large dog with him and the faithful dog attacked the thing that was trying to destroy him. The dog distracted the evil apparition long enough for the man to slip away from the gate and run home, leaving the dog to its fate. The next morning his dog returned home in a terrible state, with not a hair left on its body, and shortly afterwards died. Unsurprisingly, local people were not keen to go through the gate after dark.

Some time after this event happened there was another incident involving the Beard Gateway. This happened in February, when a group of people were returning home from a fair or market in Ballygrant (incidentally, people from Bridgend say that 'Ballygrant' comes from the Gaelic for 'ugly town'). Travelling in the cold and gathering dark, the group were easily distracted into a wayside inn.

One member of the company, Ewan McCorkindale, had to pass the Bearded Gateway and the haunted dell to get home. After a few drams, the others were teasing him – was he not afraid he might encounter the *bodach* (old man) or the *cailleach* (old woman) going through the gate? After a few drams, Ewan declared that he was not bothered; in fact he rashly said 'I will drink a health to the *bodach* but the *cailleach* can go to the dogs!'

Weaving his way home he found the area around the dell to be covered in a low mist or freezing fog that seemed to swirl around the gate. Out of the mist and dark came two apparitions – a *bodach* and a *cailleach*. The *cailleach* immediately tried to attack him but the *bodach* intervened and protected him. Three times this happened before the *cailleach* reluctantly withdrew with horrible hissing and screeching, her malevolent staring red eyes fixed on Ewan as she slowly disappeared. The *bodach* advised Ewan that he should go to a certain smithy, renowned for special metalwork (see page 127), explain what had happened and ask them to make him a 'protective dirk', for the *bodach* warned him that he would certainly be attacked again.

Ewan did exactly that, and indeed for a few years became known as 'Ewan of the dirk'. As long as he carried that dirk it seemed that he was safe from harm, even near the Beard Gateway at night. However,

one day he was busy harvesting near the gate and left his jacket and the dirk lying on a stook. The sun went down and he carried on working in the light of the full moon. Suddenly the *cailleach* appeared and leapt between Ewan and his dirk. Without the dirk he was vulnerable and she attacked him, squeezing his body so tight that blood spurted out of his mouth. Her own mouth was beginning to expand horribly and Ewan was drifting out of consciousness when the *bodach* appeared and managed to chase her away.

Unfortunately, the *bodach* had come too late to protect him. The *bodach* gave Ewan his dirk back and told him to go home and take to bed. If he could last through until cock-crow, the *bodach* told him he would enjoy five more years of life. Ewan stumbled home, in great pain, and his family looked after him through the night. The night seemed long as the full moon slowly traversed the sky. A couple of times Ewan woke and asked if the cock had crowed yet. It had not, and indeed, before the herald of the dawn could stir itself to crow on the dungheap, Ewan had passed away.

The Haunted Bridge

At the south end of Islay, there is a bridge between Laphroaig and Lagavulin which is supposedly haunted by the ghost of a late-night reveller who stumbled, fell into the stream and drowned. Local people do not like to walk over this bridge at night by themselves. (From C. Gordon Booth – *An Islay Notebook*)

CORMAC AND THE GOLDEN BARLEY BROOCH

It was a fine day in early May when the mysterious visitor landed his boat at the pier. Almost immediately, the local children and fisher-folk began to gather, curious about the strangely dressed stranger and his unusual vessel. After making some enquiries of the people standing around he secured his boat and made his way to the castle of the King, just beyond the edge of the town. He knocked at the gate and asked for an audience with the King.

Cormac, King of Ireland, had already watched from the battlements as the stranger strode along the path and was sufficiently intrigued that he agreed to meet with him. The stranger, who had the bearing of a warrior or perhaps a Prince, thought Cormac, greeted the King with confidence, while yet conveying all due respect, much in the way that diplomats are trained to do. Cormac was interested in the fine clothes the visitor wore, perfectly tailored wool and soft leather, and over his shoulders a long cloak of bright crimson, with a cinnamon brown lining.

Cormac was especially attracted to the brooch of glittering gold that pinned the cloak to his shoulder. The brooch was in the shape of three ears of barley, with the finest, most delicate strands of gold forming the whiskers of the grain. As the stranger moved the brooch would occasionally shake, giving an elusive impression of tinkling music. Cormac politely asked his guest where he had journeyed from and the man replied, 'I come from an island, not far from here; a land where only the truth is spoken, where happiness reigns and where sorrow, envy, hatred or evil do not exist.'

Cormac had taken an immediate liking to this newcomer and told him that he was welcome at the court, could stay as long as he wished, and that he and his servants would try to make him feel rested after his journey. At that, Cormac called for a serving boy to bring mead and cakes so that they could take some refreshment together. While they were carousing and relaxing, Cormac asked about the curious brooch which he had been admiring ever since the stranger arrived. The visitor explained that barley was considered extremely important in the island that was his home and that it inspired much in the way of art, storytelling and music.

Cormac, even more intrigued, asked for some examples. The stranger told the ancient ballad of John Barleycorn, which Cormac had never heard and then gently shook the strands of the barley brooch at the serving boy who instantly fell asleep. Cormac himself began to drift off into a pleasant slumber but then found the stranger touching him on the shoulder and offering him a drink of some golden liquid he had produced from a flask made of deer horn. This liquid was made from barley, by skilled alchemists, he explained, and could bring sleep, truth or joy, depending on one's needs. Cormac drank and suddenly understood why the barley was held in such high esteem by the visitor and his people.

Emboldened by this liquid that seemed to bring the very sun to his lips and fire to his belly, Cormac asked if he might have the golden brooch as a gift. The stranger, aware of the unwritten rules of hospitality, could not but agree. However, he asked in return that Cormac should grant him three wishes. Cormac, equally aware of the principles of reciprocity, also agreed, even though the wishes were not specified. As King of Ireland he felt confident that he would be able to oblige whatever the stranger might ask; in any case he was now determined he must have the magical brooch. Cormac immediately put on the barley brooch and went around the castle, amused and amazed to see how the entire household fell asleep whenever they heard the tinkling music of the golden barley beards.

It was exactly a year later that the handsome young Prince returned to Cormac's castle. Cormac's spirits were already high from the bright colours of spring, the lengthening days and the warmth of the sun. When he saw his new friend, this time wearing a cloak as heart-breakingly green as the freshest first leaves of beech, he was delighted and made a fuss of him, calling for the finest fare and jugs of mead. After some merry-making (including the visitor's golden liquid), Cormac asked if he had come to claim his three wishes. The Prince bowed respectfully and said, 'Yes, and if it please your Highness, my first wish is to ask for your daughter's hand in marriage.'

Actually Cormac was delighted by this request, thinking that a better match for his daughter would be hard to find and also that forming links with this interesting land across the sea would do his Kingdom

no harm. He agreed immediately. The women of the Royal Court were not so sure, however, and began to grumble questions and doubts — who was this stranger, what was his lineage, the extent of his land and wealth, and where would their beloved Princess be going? Cormac simply shook the golden barley brooch and the music made them fall asleep.

Another year passed and the May Day came round bringing happiness and lightness of spirit to the people of Cormac's castle and Kingdom and once again the warrior Prince appeared. This time he was wearing a cloak of grey, like the gathering dusk, but with a lining of pink and gold that flashed like the boldest sunset. Once more he and Cormac caroused, exchanged drams and told stories. This time, the visitor announced that his second wish was to be granted guardianship of Cormac's youngest son, Cairbre. Once again, Cormac agreed, feeling that the boy would learn much and would have the company of his older sister in his new home. This time, however, the women of the household grumbled even more loudly for the boy was a favourite of the court. Cormac simply shook the golden barley broach and they immediately fell into a smiling sleep.

Another year turned round through the seasons till the song-birds of May celebrated life loudly in the blue skies above Cormac's Kingdom. The handsome Prince returned, his cloak now in colours of pearl and silver, like the moon and the stars, with a lining of midnight, charcoal black. Cormac had a sense of anxiety this time, and rightly so, for it turned out that the visitor's third wish was to take Cormac's wife home with him. Cormac was not in the least bit happy about this but he felt honour-bound to keep his promise.

However, as the Prince walked away with his cloak around the shoulders of Cormac's wife, she glanced back and her look of pleading and grief was too much for Cormac to bear. He ordered a band of his warriors to get ready and they set off in pursuit. They raced to the haven and prepared the King's ship with all haste while Cormac watched the stranger's boat sail towards the northern horizon. As soon as they were able to change from oars to sails and properly get underway, a thick mist arose, as if from nowhere, hiding the other vessel from their view. The best they could do was to hold to the course they had set and proceed hopefully.

Before long, they came to a land fringed by long sandy beaches with high dunes behind. Beyond the dunes stretched a sweet moorland of heathers, herbs and flowers with many birds, insects and wild creatures everywhere. They saw attractive, comfortable houses all around and the people seemed bright-eyed and friendly. Here and there they could see whitewashed buildings with curious, broad chimney vents, from which fragrant smoke drifted across the moor and down towards the sea. The distant purple mountains seemed majestic.

Enquiring about the Lord of the land, they were politely directed to a fine castle. The large gates were open and they entered the courtyard; here was a perfect circle of nine lush hazel trees and in the middle a silver pool. Plump hazelnuts hung from the trees even though it was only May. Whenever any of these brown nuts fell into the pool, they were snapped up by five large salmon swimming around and around. Five small streams radiated away from the pool and the sound of the water was like a musical harmony of everlasting joy.

Proceeding to the great hall, Cormac and his men saw two figures seated on thrones of oak. One was an elderly man of regal bearing and the other was a beautiful woman whose age could not be guessed. Cormac was hailed and welcomed as if expected and invited to soak in a bath of warm water. As he did this he felt the warmth of the fragrant bath ease away his cares and concerns.

Just as Cormac finished bathing, a broad-shouldered man came in to the hall carrying an axe, a log and a small pig. With the axe, he split the log in pieces and then killed the pig. He lit a fire of the split log (though Cormac noticed that the wood never seemed to be consumed by the fire) and put a pot of water over the fire to boil. Dividing the pig into quarters he placed them in the pot, saying, 'The food will be ready as soon as four true stories have been told.'

Cormac, invited to tell the first tale, gave an account of how he had lost his daughter, his son and his wife as a result of the deal with the barley brooch and how he had set off in hope of finding them. Then the broad-shouldered man explained how he had found an odd-looking cow wandering and had put it in his barn. A stranger came to claim it and offered him the magic axe and log in return for the beast. He told how the log, once split, will burn forever and then, if struck with the back of the axe, becomes whole again.

The beautiful woman told the others that she had but seven cows and seven sheep, yet the milk from the cows and the wool from the sheep was enough to feed and clothe all the people in her land. Finally, the kingly man produced a golden cup which he said would split in three pieces if a lie were told but would join together again if truth was spoken. At that, the broad-backed man announced that the meal was ready. While servants proceeded to lay the table, the Lord of the castle invited them to take a drink from the golden cup. Cormac immediately recognised the taste of the warming spirit but then the beautiful woman began to sing. The song captivated Cormac's entire attention, so heavenly and haunting was the sound of her voice and the pure melody.

The song seemed to send Cormac into a swoon and when it finished and he came to his senses he was seated at a large banqueting table with his hosts opposite and his entourage on either side of him, including his wife, his son and his daughter. Cormac was overjoyed and embraced them all. The feasting began and everyone had cups of the fiery barley liquid. As the Lord opposite him drank from his golden cup, it seemed to Cormac that he grew younger before his eyes and suddenly he realised that it was none other than the warrior Prince who had come to his castle on a May morning some years before.

This man could see that Cormac had many questions to ask and proceeded to explain to him. Firstly, he said something about Cormac that was clearly not true and the golden cup fell apart. Then he said, 'Cormac, I can assure you that since they left your castle, your daughter and your wife have not seen the face of a man and your son has not seen the face of a woman.' Suddenly, the pieces of the cup pinged together with a bright musical ring and the cup was once again completely whole.

The Lord continued, 'I am Manannan, son of Lir, Lord of the Sea and I sent the mist to guide you here. I wanted you to see a land of promise and perfection to guide you in your future kingship. Now I give you the golden cup of truth to go along with the barley brooch that brings peace, contentment and sleep. These added to your great wisdom will ensure that you rule your land well. In my courtyard the silver pool represents the fount of all knowledge while the five streams are the human senses of sight, hearing, smell, taste and touch. I invite you to drink from all of these now that your wisdom might be even greater and that you might achieve all the things you desire.'

Once Cormac had drunk from the streams and the silver pool, Manannan clapped his hands and musicians began playing a last song, which was an enchanted lullaby. All the guests fell asleep and when Cormac awoke, he was back in his own bed, next to his loving wife. He was wondering if it had all been an exquisite dream when he turned and saw the golden cup and the golden barley brooch lying on the dresser beside his bed. Cormac wisely ruled his kingdom for many years after and his people, especially once he taught them how to make the golden barley drink, were content and free from any annoyance.

THE ANGEL WHO MADE WINGS

Many years ago there lived, a rich merchant who also owned a distillery and lived on Islay. His wealth was talked about by the local people almost as much as his cruelty for he was known as a ruthless and stony-hearted individual. He was also a very God-fearing man in the hypocritical way that pitiless people often are.

This rich merchant reached a time in his life when he decided he should have a wife and children, for he shrank from the idea of his wealth not being passed on to heirs. As he went around the island, he was quietly searching for the right woman to take on this role.

Travelling by the shores of Loch Indaal one day, he met a poor fisherman and his sweetheart. The merchant spoke with them a while and soon realised that the fisherman's beautiful fiancée was the one he wanted; indeed if there was any love in his flinty heart, her beauty and gentle demeanour stirred it up.

A few days later, he offered the girl's parents a large and impressive dowry in return for her hand. The parents were obviously keen on this match, and even the poor fisherman, realising that he had no power in the situation and that in any case he could never provide for a wife in the way that the merchant could, did nothing to stand in the way.

The whisky merchant married his young bride, but though she was polite and obedient, her heart was never able to forget her poor fisherman and she could never grow to love the merchant. He, on the other hand, not being used to being denied, began to desire and crave her love more and more. Frequently she sat at the window of her large house watching as the fisherman walked to and from the harbour, and at night she would often weep on her pillow, whispering his name.

Over the years, the merchant grew more and more disappointed and frustrated with his wife's refusal to accept his love. One night he overheard her whisper the fisherman's name through her tears and his heart suddenly hardened and his natural cruelty and anger exploded. He made his wife a terrible final offer and ultimatum, 'If you can steal my soul by the morning, I shall be turned to stone and you will be free. But if you fail, you must stay here, and love me as you now love him.'

Unable to see any other way out of her predicament, she agreed. As darkness approached, she wondered how she might manage to steal the merchant's soul. As the moon rose, she saw her true love, the fisherman, pass by on his way home from landing fish at the harbour. She called out to him, saying, 'My Love, bring your catch to me at midnight, and I might be able to find a way for us to be together.'

The puzzled fisherman agreed and at midnight he brought all his catch to her; silvery fish glistening in the white light of the moon. All night long the girl gutted the fish and scraped the scales into a bowl. With great skill and patience, she sewed the thousands of scales into a beautiful dress and pair of wings.

As dawn was brightening the morning sky, she put on the dress and stood with arms out-stretched to catch the rays of the rising sun. The whisky merchant came into the room and, believing her to be a shining angel of the Lord, come to lead him to Heaven, fell to his knees and offered his soul to her. When the girl revealed her true self he turned to stone and she was able to be with the one she had always loved. Of course, they lived happily ever after, and eventually, when she died, she became the chief angel in charge of looking after the Islay distilleries, making sure that the other angels enjoy their share without bringing any disrespect to their kind.

THE BRIDEGROOM'S FUNERAL

A long time ago, when they first started making wonderful whisky on Islay, a beautiful young woman from near Kildalton was promised in marriage to an older but wealthy farmer. Unfortunately she was, at the same time, in love with a young distillery worker who had no land or wealth. The young distillery worker confided his dilemma to his boss, saying that if he only had the means to finance an impressive wedding feast, he would marry the girl himself.

The distillery owner, a generous man who was very fond of the young lad, offered him 35 gallons of whisky. With this gift, the youth was able to put on a wedding feast that lasted a whole month and became the stuff of legend itself, being talked about and fondly remembered for many years.

Shortly afterwards, the young couple were out walking by the shore when a small whirlwind or eddy came from the sea. As it passed close by him, the young husband was seized by a terrible sickness and died. As he lay in his wife's arms, dying, she cried out 'If the dead have any feelings at all, you will not be absent long from our bed.'

The very night after his funeral, he appeared by his wife's bedside. Telling her not to be alarmed, he told her that when the eddy had passed he had been taken by the Lady of the Emerald Isle across the sea, who was desperate to learn the secrets of making whisky. He told his wife that he would never tell the secret and that therefore other eddies might appear. If she could throw a dirk into any of these whirlwinds, shouting 'Uisque Beatha!' she might be able to get him back.

For days the young wife walked up and down the Kildalton shore. Eventually, she saw a similar eddy of wind twisting ashore from the sea. As it passed her she jumped up and threw a dirk into it, as she had been told. Immediately the whirlwind vanished and her husband dropped at her feet.

The wife sent for her relatives and showed them that her husband was back. They were finding it all a bit difficult to believe but he explained that he had been captured by the fairy people, and it really was him standing in front of them. He told them to dig up the grave if they didn't believe him. That was what they did and all they found in the coffin were a few staves of oak.

Eventually, the Lady of the Emerald Isle did discover the secrets of making whisky and after that no more whirlwinds were seen on the Islay shore. No-one knows who was taken and persuaded to divulge the secrets. The truth is partially reflected in the Irish legend that it was St Patrick who taught them the secret skills of distillation – and as we all know, Patrick was actually from Scotland. It may be that some kidnapped distiller from Islay was so venerated by the Irish that they made him their patron Saint.

THE DEVIL DANCED A JIG ON
BRUICHLADDICH PIER

The Devil may not be prepared to come to Islay, for his own personal reasons, but he still bears a grudge and from time to time tries to make mischief for the islanders, especially the distillers, in revenge for the fright he got the last time he was there (see the *Maid of Islay*, p 67). An example of one of his fiendish plans came to light in 2007 and 2008. This was a time when whisky sales were booming, all the Islay distilleries were working, new ones were being built and production was being universally cranked up; the Devil didn't like this at all, so he threw a hellish spanner in the works.

His first attempt was to quietly create conditions around the world that would result in serious increases to the price of oil. The distilleries on Islay all depend on oil for energy and Auld Nick thought he was clever doing this because he could cause trouble for Islay and its distilleries, without having to actually go there. However, though oil prices went very high indeed and did cause some problems, the Devil failed to realise that when human misery increases, the thing people automatically turn to is whisky.

Beelzebub decided he had to do more and so he gathered a few of his imps, demons and hellish henchmen and laid out his plan. First of all he sent one of his seductive influencers, Megatron, to Brussels to convince officials at the European Union that big is beautiful and environmentally friendly. They passed a law that said all oil tankers must be big – no small oil tankers could now be used anywhere. The oil companies did not complain because they always like to have new toys to play with and the bigger the better.

Word came to Islay that unless they built a new pier, harbour or other facility to accommodate these large vessels then they would have to start drilling to see if there was any oil below the peat. Lucifer then sent a team of mischief imps and a minor demon called Misinformatus to visit the officials at Argyll and Bute Council to ensure that they did not listen to reason or logic and chose the least effective option as a response to the tanker problem. With local authorities in Scotland this is really not a difficult thing to do and the Devil has ample experience of making that kind of mischief, all across the land.

Designs were then hastily put together for a bolted-on, uni-purpose extension to the Bruichladdich pier. Bruichladdich pier was the obvious choice because it is near the oil storage depot; however, that flimsy bit of logic was the only sensible part of the whole plan. Local people were consulted in the usual way, which means that there was never any chance of them being listened to. Locals were not entirely dismayed therefore, but still irritated when their reasonable suggestions (that the tankers could unload in the middle of Loch Indaal and the fuel be piped ashore, that a decent sized breakwater could be built with all the stone blasted out of the recent Port Askaig redevelopment, or that the pier should at least be designed so that other vessels could use it when tankers were not visiting) were all ignored.

The pier went up at a cost of £3.25 million pounds. Then Satan really got to work with his army of demons. First of all he sent one of his subterranean ogre-spirits, Sedimentor, to mysteriously raise the sea bed under the berthing point at the pier. The new, double sized tankers found that they could only dock if they had their tanks half empty. This rather defeated the point of having larger tankers in the first place – clever Prince of Darkness. Next he sent a maniacal mechanic, Derivetus, to loosen the ties that held the new structure to the old pier. At the same time he sent Squallus, the infernal wind-whipper to ensure that whenever the tanker appeared, strong winds would blow from the west (actually, they didn't need to be that strong – thanks

to Derivetus, the normal prevailing winds would have done the job, but Mephistopheles leaves nothing to chance).

As an extra piece of mischief, just because he could do it, Auld Clootie also enlisted the help of an aerial tribe of Moonpullers to ensure that the tides would be disrupted from time to time. The end result was that the regular tanker, *Keewhit* (if ever there was a serpent tongue-in-cheek name, this is it – reverse the sound of the name and it becomes 'whit quay?') was never able to dock and unload its fuel. The oil soon ran out and the distilleries had to stop production. The Earl of Hell was slapping his scaly thighs with glee.

Here was an island in shame and desperation. Islay had such a long history of dealing with the sea – from the Viking adventurers to the Lords of the Isles who created a veritable maritime highway, from the lighthouse builders to the famed

puffers of old, Islay had always devised ways of coping with their oceanic isolation, but now they were defeated by a simple piece of marine engineering gone wrong; jinxed! A straightforward structure, built for a single purpose, yet seemingly as useless as a chocolate teapot. There was much weeping and wailing and gnashing of teeth — just the kind of thing that Old Hornie thrives on.

The distillery managers of Islay called an emergency meeting of the Condenser Club to see what might be done. There was a fair amount of mutual suspicion because they were all afraid that one of the group might be a spy acting on behalf of Mahoun, and after all one or two of them do have the look. In the end, they could only see two possible options (they had long ago given up trying to talk sense to Argyll and Bute Council).

The first plan was to go back to the days of the puffers (someone had heard that the *Vital Spark* was lying idle at Crinan). This idea was rejected because it would need too much capital investment to return to coal-fired stills and in any case, distillery workers had developed an aversion to shovels over the years. Though it was not actually mentioned by any of them, a few also feared that the Devil would find it easy to hide in coal deliveries and might return to Islay with devastating consequences.

The second plan was to plead with the ferry operator to allow additional large vehicles onto their ferries, so that oil could come to the island by road. The distillers were very reluctant to do this, because they did not like the idea of the ferry operator (whom they normally refer to as Nosferiatus) having them over a barrel, whether a whisky barrel or an oil barrel. However, there was no alternative, and so oil was brought to the desperate distilleries of Islay by lorries driving on to ferries — the most expensive, unreliable and environmentally unfriendly possibility of all.

No-one was happy, the price of Islay whisky started to rise and the real danger was that the Devil's favoured people, the Speysiders, might have been able to take advantage and increase their share of the market. However, for any realistic chance that that could happen, they would have to start making peaty whiskies, which indeed one or two of them did. No, instead the greedy Speysiders just jumped on the bandwagon and put their prices up too. The only ones who revelled in this situation were His Satanic Majesty and his old buddy Kalmak, sitting by the fire in Hell, laughing fiendishly and enjoying a good dram together.

THE FLAGON OF THE FAIRY QUEEN

Just along the coast from Ardbeg is a conical hill called Cnoc Rhaonastil. It is an unusual geological feature; a dolorite intrusion of basalt magma, bearing interesting minerals. A pair of standing stones nearby are supposed to represent the grave of a giant Princess (some say from Denmark, some say Ireland) who travelled over the sea on stepping stones that she laid down as she went; she grew tired at Islay and drowned there. She was called Iula or Yula and supposedly gave her name to the island. It is said that people who were foolish enough to try to open her enchanted burial place have not only failed but have gone mad as a result.

Cnoc Rhaonastil is also the resting place of Talbot Clifton, a legendary figure who was laird of Kildalton between 1922 and 1928. Talbot and his equally eccentric wife, Violet, led very unusual lives and lived in some style at the nearby Kildalton Castle (built by distiller John Ramsay) which now lies in ruins. Many of their adventures and misadventures are related in Violet's book *The Book of Talbot*. Talbot used to play his flute by the shore to entertain the seals in the bay. Shortly after his death, the estate passed to his son Harry, who sold it off soon after. Harry, incidentally, also married a woman called Violet, an American who was pastor of an occult church (the Agabeg Temple); she was known as the Ghost of Hollywood and acted as spiritual consultant to some of the stars of the silver screen.

Cnoc Rhaonastil has long been identified by local people as a fairy hill and there is a specific legend associated with it. A version of this legend is found in a book by Fiona Macleod translated into German as *Wind und Woge* (Wind and Waves). Fiona Macleod was actually a *nom de plume* assumed by William Sharp, a prolific Victorian author and member of the Hermetic Society of the Golden Dawn.

The legend tells the story of how the Fairy Queen who lived under the hill sent an invitation to the women of the Isles to come to visit her at Cnoc Rhaonastil. The Fairy Queen knew how difficult life could be for the women of Islay and she decided to share with them, and indeed with the women of all the islands, some of the fairy wisdom, for in the world of fairies it is the women who look after the cup from which wisdom is dispensed.

The invitation went out to every island off the coast of Scotland, carried by the winds, the birds and the fish of the sea. The reaction among the women who heard it was varied; some did not believe or trust what they thought they had heard. Some were intrigued but could not imagine how they could make the journey; some were insulted that the fairies thought they might have anything to teach them and others were even afraid that it might be some kind of trick, for the fairies did have a reputation for outwitting humans, and even occasionally kidnapping them. Nonetheless, there were many who saw an opportunity not to be missed and started to make arrangements. The more the women of the islands talked among themselves about this invitaion, the more that view came to prevail.

On the day specified in the Fairy Queen's invitation, the weather was bright and breezy, perfect for those who had decided to make the journey, and soon the horizon was filled with sails of every colour as boats of all sizes began to approach Islay. The women who arrived were astonished to see the hill open up and with a mixture of awe and trepidation they went inside. The women gazed in amazement at everything they saw in the Fairy Queen's hall, and of course they had a particular eye for the tapestries and coverings which were all done in the finest, neatest weaving, stitching and embroidery possible. They could hardly imagine anyone doing work so detailed and artistic as that.

Even the colours were unlike anything they had seen, for the fairies had clearly developed the skill of extracting dye from all sorts of plants. There were many purples, from the palest heather and violet shades, through to the darkest hues of blackberries and elder. There were orangy reds from the berries of rowan (the name Rhaonastil means rowan dell) and blood reds from raspberry, for these are the kind of colours the fairies love. But the colours that drew most gasps were the greens; greens of a bright, vibrant nature which must have been magically taken from youngest, freshest leaves of spring, with the light of a sunny day trapped inside, to the earthy dark greens of winter holly and everything in between.

This fantasy of light and shade was further enhanced by the myriad lights. Here and there scented candles burned, some glass jars seemed to contain fireflies, delicate lamps and chandeliers hung on slender threads from the high ceiling and crystals sent out beams of light that dazzled. These crystals seemed to reflect shafts of sunshine that came down from holes high in the corners of the hall. The crystals revolved by some magic, so that as the sun and the sunbeams moved with the advancing hours, the prism still caught and threw out shards of light.

The women had been welcomed warmly by the fairy folk and many of them were asking their hosts questions about the things they saw around them. A fabulous banquet was laid and the table was glittering with ornaments of finest metal, place mats of beautifully carved slate, plates of turned wood and drinking goblets of stone, glass and shell; the women admired and feasted their eyes but they knew it was not yet the time to sit down. Then came the sound of distant voices in fabulous harmonised chanting, the words alien but beautiful; the sound grew slowly louder and then the Fairy Queen made her entrance.

Humans often refer to the fairy folk as the Little People and we have an idea of them being smaller than us. Whether some trick had made the women smaller entering the hall or whether fairies are not all the same size, certainly there was nothing diminutive about the Fairy Queen. She was a creature of impressive appearance, very regal and clearly someone used to her position of unquestioned authority. Her features were ageless and beautiful; the light of the room and its many green colours reflected in her eyes. Her clothes were magnificent but comfortable, not with the weight and cumbersome grandeur of human queens of old and she was every bit as tall as most of the women gathered there.

At a gesture from the Queen, the women were brought to the table by the fairy helpers and the banquet was served. The women of the isles found that each had a fairy friend on either side and they were encouraged to ask as many questions as they liked of their hosts. The fairies asked questions in return, though some of the time, unless the questions were for personal information, the more astute women had the feeling that their hosts already knew the answers. Finally, the Fairy Queen rose to address the guests and told them of her purpose in inviting them to her Hall. She explained that she hoped they might leave this place holding more answers than questions and how she wished that might be a principle of life that they could enjoy thereafter passing it on to their daughters and sharing it, as much as possible, with the women who had been unable or unwilling to come to Cnoc Rhaonastil.

Then she lifted a flagon from the table in front of her, telling them that this vessel contained a precious golden liquid that was the distilled wisdom of the world, acquired over the years by countless generations of fairy women and carefully guarded by the queen herself. She then passed among them pouring some of the precious liquid into each cup. There were many cups to fill but the flagon never seemed to empty and there was easily enough to go around. The Queen raised her cup and made a toast in the fairy tongue and all the women raised their cups and drank. The stuff they drank had a fiery touch to the lips and a warmth that trickled all the way down as they swallowed it. After a few moments of enjoying the warm glow, the women became aware of a sense of calm and confidence that seemed to suffuse their bodies and their minds; silence reigned for a while as it seemed that no-one had the need to ask questions any more.

After many warm words of thanks and farewell, the women prepared to leave the Hall and return to their homes on Islay or across the sea. When they came out into the sunshine they found a small group of women from the mainland who had somehow got word of the invitation and had made the journey hopefully. However, they had arrived too late as the wind had been against them and they had to go home without the benefit of the gift of wisdom from the flagon of the Fairy Queen. Once in a while, the women of the Isles have been known to talk about their mainland sisters (or even island sisters who do things slightly out of character) and say, how unfortunate, that they were not there when the wisdom cup was passed around.

THE HOUSE OF BLISS

Every island has its misty, Celtic fable of a heavenly place where perfection is found, where lucky travellers sometimes stray, to their amazement and delight and where wounded soldiers or those sick at heart are sometimes magically transported. In that special place they find solace, companionship, humanity and peace; wounds are healed and broken hearts made whole.

These magic, Avalon-like places are not on any map, and those who are lucky enough to encounter them are usually never able to find their way back. Mostly, in Celtic legend, such places are controlled by women, often mythical creatures with supernatural abilities, including the ability to change shape and to assume the form of animals and birds.

There is such a place on Islay, known as 'the House of Bliss'. No-one knows where it is, though the legends usually place it on the Rinns. The woman who lives there is a shadowy beauty, thought to be some princess from a foreign land, who is sometimes seen on or near the shore, where she is a seal or *silkie*, and sometimes hopping around on a rock in the form of a small bird. Locals refer to this unusual bird as the 'wren with a long beak', but this may be an English corruption of the French *reine de l'alembic* (queen of the stills).

I have been fortunate enough to visit Islay's House of Bliss, though I am not able to give its exact location. My memory of the experience however, gives me lasting comfort. I remember a place where dry peats burn on an open fire with mesmerising blue and yellow flames, where a fabulous range of whiskies is freely available, where enchanting, delicate music is played and where intelligent conversation stimulates the soul.

When the weary traveller has been satisfied with all these things and the almost magical food that is presented, he or she can be soothed under warm rain in a spacious, heavenly shower and finally fall asleep on a soft bed. Above the bed is a roof full of windows, through which can be seen the moon and stars performing their slow, stately waltz around the 'bonnie brookit bairn' that is our planet.

Was it real or was it a blissful dream?

THE LEGEND OF THE SMITH
AND THE FAIRIES

Years ago, there lived on Islay a blacksmith named MacEachern. MacEachern had a 13 year old son, who was cheerful, strong and healthy. Suddenly, the boy fell ill and took to his bed for weeks. No one could discover what was the matter with him, but he seemed to be wasting away, growing thin, wrinkly and yellow, and his father and friends were afraid he might die.

The boy lay in this condition for a long time, getting neither better nor worse, but yet with an extraordinary appetite. One day, while sadly reflecting on this, standing idly at his forge with no will to work, the smith was agreeably surprised to see an old man, well known for his wisdom and knowledge of strange things, approaching the smithy. MacEachern poured the visitor a dram of his best and told him of the strange matter that was clouding their lives.

The old man listened seriously and after sitting a while appreciating his dram and considering what he had heard, he ventured an opinion. 'I believe it is not your son that you have, but that the fairies have carried him away and left you a *Sibhreach* in his place.'

'Alas!' said the smith, 'What on earth can I do? Have you any idea how to help?' The old man indicated that he might and was immediately encouraged by having his dram topped up.

'First, to make sure that is not your son, take as many empty egg shells as you can get into the room and spread them out carefully in front of him. Then proceed to draw water with them, carrying them in your hands, as if they were a great weight, and arrange them when full, with every sort of earnestness round the fire.' The smith, therefore, gathered as many egg shells as he could find and proceeded to carry out these instructions. He had not been at it long, when a shout of laughter arose from the bed and the voice of the apparently sick boy exclaimed, 'Well! I've lived 800 years and I have never seen anything like that!'

The smith returned to the old man, whose glass was now once again empty, and told him what he had heard. 'Aha!' said the sage, 'Clearly that is not your son. Your boy must be with the fairies in the fairy mound at Borra-chiel. If you would be so good as to pour me another of these fine drams, I'll tell you what to do next.' The smith readily agreed.

The old man continued, 'You must light a huge bright-burning fire in front of the bed on which this stranger is lying. When he asks what you are doing, tell him to look closer and then grab him and throw him into the flames. If it is your son, he will call out for you to save him, but if not, the thing will fly away.'

The smith again followed the old man's advice, kindled a large fire, answered the boy as directed and then, seizing the child, flung him straight into the heart of the fire. The *Sibhreach* gave a spine-chilling shriek and disappeared through the smoke hole in the roof.

MacEachern was now desperate to get

his true son back and gladly poured the old man yet another dram. When he heard what he had to do next, he poured himself a large one too. The visitor told him he had to go to the fairy mound at Borra-chiel on a certain night when access would be possible. The smith was to approach the hill carrying a bible, a dirk and a crowing cock. There would be sounds of merriment and dancing and at midnight he would be able to find the open door by the light blazing through it.

On entering the hill he was to jam the dirk in the entrance to prevent the door closing and to proceed with confidence, as the bible would protect him from any harm. The old man told him to go right to the centre of the room. His son would probably be working at the forge on the far side and when questioned he was to announce his intention not to leave without the boy.

That is how things happened, though in truth, when the smith heard the sound of many voices and bagpipes coming from the hill at midnight, he became extremely anxious. Nonetheless he went boldly in. The fairies were grim and threatening but they shrank back from the bible. When he called out loudly that he would not leave without his son all the fairies burst out laughing in a raucous, evil shout. The noise woke the sleeping cock, which had been hidden under MacEachern's coat; it jumped up on the smith's shoulders, flapped its wings and crowed loud and long. Immediately, the fairies disappeared and all the lights went out. The smith and his son were able to get through the door, but on removing the dirk the door slammed shut and seemed to become merely part of the hillside.

MacEachern took his son home and sent for the old man, whom he shook firmly and gratefully by the hand before pouring him the biggest ever dram in the history of Islay. He had long been aware of the value of drams for cementing friendships but he now also realized the power of whisky to provide the inspiration for solving thorny problems.

Though rescued, the son was withdrawn and distant for a year and a day, as if under some shadow. Then, while watching his father work on a particularly intricate piece of metalwork on the hilt of a sword for some important chief, he suddenly jumped up, saying, 'That's not how to do it,' and taking the weapon from his father, worked on it quickly and skilfully, turning out the finest sword ever seen in the whole country.

From then on, the son and the father worked closely as a team and the name of MacEachern spread far and wide as the finest metalworkers and weapon makers in all the islands. They lived together for many years, enjoying wealth and happiness in equal measure.

This story is from the J. F. Campbell collection. Here are some other variations.

The Young Man in the Fairy Knoll

Two young men were walking home in the dark one Halloween, each carrying a large jar of whisky. On the way they saw what appeared to be a house of some kind with lights blazing and sounds of music and merriment. Perhaps emboldened by having had a few drams they went in.

One of the lads immediately got into the party mode and started dancing with the folk in the house. The second man was slightly more cautious than his friend and didn't exactly like the look of the people in there or indeed the strange dwelling they had arrived at. He went in too, but left his kilt pin jammed in the door and would not join in the dance. Eventually he decided to leave and tried to persuade his friend to come too. The friend seemed to be enjoying himself too much and wanted to stay. As soon as he removed the pin and came outside the dwelling disappeared and there was only a dark, silent knoll.

Exactly a year later he returned to the same place and once again found the lighted house with sounds of riotous fun coming out. Once again he jammed something in the door and went in. There was his friend still dancing away. He practically had to drag his friend away but finally pulled him out of the place; yet again the lights went out. Once he got his friend on the outside, it became clear that he had wasted away to being little more than skin and bone and he was lucky to survive. The story does not say what happened to the whisky!

Johnnie in the Cradle

There was a wee bairn in this particular family that seemed to change; he started greeting all the time. The parents didn't know what was wrong and nothing they could do seemed to make any difference.

The father was a farmer and one Saturday he and his wife had to go to the market so they asked a neighbour who was a tailor if he would look after the greeting bairn for a few hours.

The tailor sat down and prepared to have his lugs rattled for a while but almost as soon as the parents left, the bairn sat up and spoke, 'Is my mother and faither away?' The tailor said they were and then the bairn said to him, 'There's whisky in the press, gie's a drink.' The tailor, amazed, decided to humour the wee lad. After the bairn had taken a couple of pulls at the whisky jug, he announced that he would like to have a blow at his father's bagpipes, which were lying in the ingle nook. So the time went by and the tailor watched on as the bairn had a wee party to itself.

When the parents returned, the bairn went back to greeting in his bed. The tailor said nothing but realised that the bairn was a fairy. Later on, in private, he told the

parents what had happened. So they set up a connivance and pretended to repeat the same thing the following week. This time the farmer was listening at the window. When he heard the bairn asking for whisky he ran into the house and tried to grab it, intending to throw it on the fire. However, the fairy shrieked and flew up the lum and disappeared — without even waiting for its dram.

THE TALE OF THE SOLDIER

Once upon a time, an old soldier on his way home from an army campaign, passed through a village. Wearied with walking, he eventually came to the house of a gentleman. He knocked on the door and asked for lodgings for the night. 'Well then,' said the gentleman, 'since you are an old soldier and have the look of a man of courage, without dread or fear in your face, there is a castle at the side of the wood over there and you may stay there until daybreak. You shall have a pipe and baccy, a cogie full of whisky and a bible to read.'

When John had finished his supper he took himself off to the castle, lit a large fire in the grate and settled himself down for the night. At a certain time of the night there came in two tawny women carrying a dead man's kist, which they dropped in front of the fire and then quickly took themselves off. John got up and with the heel of his boot he drove out the end of the kist and dragged out of it a hoary old *bodach*. He sat the *bodach* in the great chair and provided him with a pipe of baccy and a cogie of whisky. The old man immediately let them fall to the floor. 'Poor man,' said John, 'you must be suffering from the cold.' John stretched himself out on the bed, leaving the old *bodach* to toast himself at the fireside. In the early hours, when the cock crowed, the old man disappeared.

Soon after, the gentleman appeared, saying, 'What rest did you find John?' 'Good rest,' said John, 'your father was not the kind of man that would frighten me.' 'Well, John, if you lie one more night in the castle, you shall have two hundred pounds.'

'I can do that fine,' said John, and the night passed in a similar way, but this time three tawny women appeared in the middle of the night, with a dead man's kist, which they dropped before the fire and then departed.

John arose, and with the heel of his boot, broke the heads of the kist, dragged out the hoary old man, and just like the night before, set him up in the great chair with a pipe and some baccy. Once again they fell from the *bodach*'s hands. 'Oh! Poor man,' said John, 'the cold is surely bothering you.' Then he gave him a cogie of whisky and he let that fall too. 'Oh! Poor man,' said John, 'Cold is a terrible thing.'

Once again, the *bodach* disappeared at cock-crow. John said to himself, 'if we meet again another night, you will pay for the pipe of baccy and cogie of drink that I have given up.'

The gentleman returned to the castle in the early morning, saying, 'What rest did you find last night, John?'

'Good rest,' said John, 'I was still not afraid of your father, the hoary old *bodach*.'

'Och!' said the gentleman, 'if you stay here tonight again, you shall have three hundred pound.'

'It's a deal,' said John.

After a while, during the night, four tawny women came in carrying the dead man's kist, which they set down in front of John.

John got up, drew his foot and kicked out the ends of the kist. He dragged out the hoary old man and propped him in the big chair. He gave him pipe, baccy and the cup of whisky, but once again the *bodach* let them fall and they were broken.

'Och!' said John, 'before you leave here you shall pay me for everything you have broken,' but of course there was no word of reply. John took the belt from his haversack and used it to tie the old man to his side, and then with the old man strapped to him he lay down on the bed. Eventually, when the heath-cock crowed, the *bodach* turned to John and asked him to let him go.

'Pay for what you have broken first.' said John.

'Well then,' said the old man, 'I will tell you something. Underneath this floor is a cellar of drink, in which there is plenty of whisky, tobacco and pipes. Next to the cellar is another little room in which you will find a cauldron full of gold and under the threshold of the big door there is a crocky full of silver. Did you see the women who came in here with me?'

'Yes, I saw them,' said John.

'Well, those were four women that I took cows from, even though they were in extremity; so every night they carry me around like this, to punish me for it. You go and tell my son how much it is wearying me out and ask him to return the cows. Tell him not to be hard on the poor. You and he can share the gold and silver between you but mind and spare plenty for the poor, on whom I was too hard, and maybe I will at last find rest.'

The gentleman came, and John told him what the *bodach* had said. Towards the end of the day, John filled his pockets with gold and reminded the gentleman to be generous to the poor; then he set off once more, on the long journey home.

John Francis Campbell collected this tale from John MacDonald, a travelling tinker.

SECTION FIVE

WHISKY HEROES

CAPTAIN GORRIE'S RIDE

Horses have been important to Islay folk for a long time. There is a saying on the island that 'an Islay man will walk a mile carrying a saddle and bridle to ride half a mile.' They love horses; in one of the Statistical Accounts from the 18th century a minister commented that there were probably too many horses on the Rinns. The Rinns is still a place where you can see fine horses grazing in fields by the road.

It is said that Moidart ponies came to Islay as spoils of war after the Battle of Culloden because Islay men fought with the Duke of Argyll on the King's side. With such importance given to horses on the island there were bound to be one or two horse legends.

The poem that tells the story of Captain Gorrie's Ride is by Thomas Pattison and is to be found in his book *Gaelic Bards*. A foot note says that the poem is 'reminiscent of a story about John McEwan, who in his younger days was a successful smuggler on the farm of his father, a respectable tenant in the Oa. John had some whisky on hand, and observing the gaugers prowling about in the gloaming, he saddled his good brown mare, and mounting, hung, Gilpin-like, a cask of pure Islay on each side, 'to make his balance true' and bolted off towards the Big Strand, through Duich sand-knolls, along the Iron Bridge, and turned off the main road and dashed up the avenue that leads up to the Lonbain farm. When John thus eluded the vigilant eyes of the Excisemen, hotly pursuing him on horseback, he feared that the 'sparks of fire which the iron heels of his spirited brown mare struck out of the hard and flinty highway' might betray his whereabouts on the road. Honest John's 'racing and chasing' was along the same route as Captain Gorrie.'

The whisky connection here is in the parallel rides of John McEwan and Captain Gorrie; one was pursued by the Excisemen, the other by the Devil. John was trying to get his casks of 'pure Islay' safe whereas Captain Gorrie's purpose is not clear. The chances are it involved either whisky or love – what else would induce him to leave 'bien and fireside' and a 'steaming jug'? Perhaps he too was transporting contraband 'pure Islay' or more likely, since the poem says it was harvest time, he had to get some barley in before it was ruined. Of course it may also be that he was doing an Islay pub crawl and had to get to the last Change House before closing time.

Captain Gorrie was in fact Captain Godfrey MacNeill, tenant of Kilcalumkil, near Port Ellen. He was the elder brother of Major Ban MacNeill of Balmory, in the Rinns. Captain Gorrie was famed as a keen sportsman and athlete and was considered the best rider in Islay. His white pony was a high-stepping, fleet-footed Highland steed. The rough and rapid ride from Kilcalumkil, four miles above Port Ellen to Carnbeg, within a mile of Port Askaig is 28 miles. He did it in one hour.

CAPTAIN GORRIE'S RIDE

Still is the night — the mist is wild,
The hour is waxing late,
The road is grey, the moor is black
And dim and desolate.

The wind it moves, its touch is soft,
Its breath is faint and low;
The damp of the wide waste hath flagged
Its heavy wing and slow.

The moon is near its setting wheeled,
And the southwest is bright;
Where half obscured, its site is marked
By a dim blotch of light.

All else is dark above, below,
And silent as the dead;
All, save the hoarse and swollen brook
That frets its moory bed.

Another sullen stifled sound,
Is the deep note and grand
That lulls in every hour of calm,
An ocean-girded land.

Ten miles the road doth stretch along
Before a house you reach;
Three miles through moor and sandhills,
And even along the beach.

Where, ever as you wander on,
The sea-waves rolling blue,
The yellow sand, the bent so brown,
And streamlets passing through.

Rocks, hills, and silent distant moors,
Are all that you may see;
But in the night 'tis lonelier far,
And wild as well may be.

Why then so late and carelessly,
On trampling steed and strong,
Rides Captain Gorrie all alone,
This lonely road along?

What boon and joyous company,
What bien and bright fireside,
Have sent him from their jovial cheer,
To take this cheerless ride?

'Twere better sure for horse and man,
To hold till morrow morn,
The steaming jug, the merry talk,
The stable and the corn.

But the Captain — it was harvest then —
The Captain thought not so;
And though the night was dim and dark,
The Captain he would go.

And ever as he onward rode,
He hummed a manly strain;
In tent and field, he used to sing,
In Asia and in Spain.

The road is long, — the Captain stern
And sterner sings the while;
'Tis a song of Fionn Mac Cu'aill,
the hero of the Gael.

And ever as he sings, he hears
The massy tread below,
Of the steed that bore him safely
Up the promontory's brow.

When the narrow rocky footway
To the old fort that led,
Rung loud with sound unwonted
Beneath his iron tread.

And the Captain he looks round and hums
More daringly and clear,
His ancient song whene'er his steed
Starts at the touch of fear.

Thus far they tell the road is lost
In the loose shifted sand,
And nearer they approach and near
The loud and roaring strand.

What ails thy steed now, Captain, tell —
What ail thy steed and thee —
What makes him start and snort so loud
At scenting of the sea?

What feeling makes him toss so high
His head, and step so light,
And seem for nervous start prepared,
And haste and headlong flight?

A strong hand holds the bridle rein,
The horse turns to the left,
And all along the line of waves
Trips warily and deft.

His rider looks a moment round,
When o'er the wide blue sea,
Before the moon that bursts its shroud
The misty shadows flee.

The gelding grey starts once again,
The Captain glances back —
My God! What stalwart horseman rides
Upon that giant black!

Dies in a cough the Captain's song,
He spurs the gallant grey,
By slow degrees he faster flees
Along the salt sea spray.

But ever as he glances round,
The jet black steed is by;
Though ne'er a breath the Captain hears,
Nor horse-hoofs beating nigh.

The motion fires the Captain's soul,
He thinks of that awful place,
Where deep and rayless darkness hold
The fallen angel race.

He thinks of him all suddenly,
In his own pathway found,
So black and grim, who rides so trim,
Without a word or sound.

And the Captain feels his heart oppressed,
And a strange terror rise,
And with a battle shout away,
Winged like the wind he flies.

But still his wild companion comes,
So dark, so dismal dread,
And louder shouts the Captain,
And faster flies his steed.

Over the hills and rivulets,
Over the holts and hags,
O'er dyke, and rock, and beaten road,
His wild course never flags —

Till at his stable door, in haste,
In heat, and disarray,
His servants find the Captain bold,
At breaking of the day.

The Captain he was weary,
But the Captain he was well,
The gallant grey was weary too,
For he stumbled and he fell,

And rolled away, and lifeless lay
With a gasp upon his side,
No more his master backs the grey,
In rough and rapid ride.

As the Captain looks in pity,
The salt tear fills his eye,
He thinks of that dread horseman,
Through all the night so nigh.

And swears to raise a monument,
And dig a noble grave,
For the horse that beat Beelzebub
Beside the salt sea wave.

DANIEL THE GREAT

'Great' Daniel Campbell, founder of the second Campbell dynasty of Islay, was actually born Donald Campbell in 1670 but later changed his name to the anglicised form of Daniel. His mother had some Islay connections and his father was the Captain of Skipness Castle in Kintyre. At the age of 15 he received the news that his uncle had been hanged in front of Inveraray Castle for taking part in the 1685 Rebellion. His father was also on a shoogly nail for a while but though he lost his lands and position he managed to stay attached to his neck.

The teenage Daniel thus found himself in need of making a fortune as he was no longer going to inherit one. Like many minor aristos of his time he turned his eyes to the New World and, in his early 20s, he sailed to New England where he purchased a merchant ship. The possibilities for trade between America and the old country were good at that time and he slowly built up a fleet of ships, carrying linen, iron ore and herring in one direction and sugar and tobacco in the other. It is clear from some of the records that he also carried slaves from time to time.

It did not take the able Daniel very long to amass a significant fortune, despite being embroiled in the most notorious and disastrous 'get rich quick' scheme of the day – the Darien Scheme. Daniel quickly used his profits to purchase the impressive homes that a hugely successful merchant would desire, the better to demonstrate his wealth and importance. In 1711 he built the Shawfield Mansion, an impressive house at the north side of the Trongate in the centre of Glasgow. From that point he became known as Daniel Campbell of Shawfield. He later acquired an even more impressive pile at Woodhall, near Holytown in Lanarkshire. Daniel lived through interesting times

– he lived through the Covenanting Killing Times, the deaths of Charles II and James II and the subsequent Glorious Revolution (1688). He was still a young man making his fortune when the Campbells secured their blackest mark in the history of Scotland – the Massacre of the Macdonalds in Glencoe (1692) and when the Darien Scheme collapsed (1698–99). He was heavily involved in the Treaty of Union in 1707, having been elected to the Scottish Parliament in 1702; in fact he was one of the signatories of the Act of Union.

He lived to see the battles of Killie-crankie, Sherrifmuir and the various attempts to restore the Stuarts, including the 1715 and the 1745 Risings and the last battle on British soil, Culloden in 1746. His was a time of great civil unrest – the Holyrood riot (1688), the Shawfield Riot (1725) and the Porteus Riots (1736). In terms of the various conflicts of the time and the way the popular imagination and folklore have dressed them up for posterity, Daniel and indeed the Campbells in general, were nearly always on the 'wrong' (i.e. the unpopular) side.

Daniel had friends in high places – he was on intimate terms with Robert Walpole – but he also had political, ideological and social detractors and enemies. George Lockhart of Carnwath, an anti-Unionist, described him as 'an arrogant grasping fellow' and Bruce Lenman called him 'a hard-faced, grasping Hanovarian Whig merchant oligarch.' A slight hint of scandal was whispered down succeeding Campbell generations, who suspected that the Shawfield Pearls, a priceless family heirloom, had been given by Daniel to an exotic foreign lady in return for certain favours.

It was the Shawfield Riot which has the most relevance to the tale of how 'Great' Daniel Campbell became the head of the dynasty that shaped Islay, its social and economic history, its towns and the remarkable Islay House. Daniel Campbell of Shawfield, MP was one of the architects of the Malt Tax of 1725. This was unpopular because the price of beer and ale would rise, in order, it was suspected, to favour imported wine and brandy.

As an importer of sugar, Daniel owned a sugar house and, in common with other people in the same trade, used the sugar for distilling. Joanna Hill, in her book *A Very Canny Scot*, reports that Daniel applied for a licence to set up a distillery in Glasgow and employed William Walker as distiller. Between 1707 and 1715 in Glasgow half a million gallons of sugar spirit were distilled. Being granted the status of a 'manufactory' allowed Daniel to conduct this activity without paying either tax or duty. Perhaps he had a vested interest in seeing tax on malt increase.

Nothing is more likely to incense a Glasgow mob than putting up the cost of their drink. The mob took to the streets and specifically targeted Campbell's mansion at Shawfield. The place was thoroughly ransacked, though the Campbell family were conveniently safe in their other mansion at Woodhall (along with many of their valuables, according to some).

The damage to the house was considerable; the mob appeared to have made for the cellars first, then looted and finally vented their inebriated spleens on the fabric of the building. Campbell himself wrote, 'They broke into my cellars which were but too well stocked for such monstrous guests.' Unfortunately, the drink may have emboldened the mob a little too much because when the militia finally got organised and tried to disperse them, they resisted and nine citizens were killed and at least 17 were injured. This did Campbell's popularity no good at all, indeed the following year a further tax had to be levied on Glasgow beer in order to fund the compensation that Daniel was to receive for the damage to his house.

It may well be that 'Great' Daniel decided it would be safer for him and his family to move somewhere quieter; that place was Islay. In fact he had already paid £6,000 to Sir John Campbell of Cawdor for lands in Islay and Jura. With the huge amount of compensation he received for the damage to Shawfield (about £9,000) he was able to buy the whole of Islay and half of Jura. So, thanks to a drunken mob complaining about this malt tax, Daniel Campbell acquired the future whisky island, that Hebridean malt heaven of Islay.

Thus began the reign of the Campbells of Shawfield in Islay. The Campbells of Cawdor and the old order were replaced by a new order that was business-like and administratively tight. According to his grandson, 'Great' Daniel Campbell 'introduced a spirit of industry into the Island of Isla, as the most proper means to Divert from, and if possible, to Eradicate Idel-Loving and Clanish Spirit that prevailed.' Needless to say, there were some on Islay who did not like the change and throughout the 18th century many people emigrated from there to the New World.

Islay House, the new ancestral seat, was extended in stages and transformed from a 17th century tower house to an enormous palace, eventually with 24 bedrooms and 365 windows. The settlement of Killarrow was transplanted to Bowmore in order that Islay House should have more private space and parkland. 'Great' Daniel planned the move, though it was Daniel the Second, his grandson who carried it out after he inherited the estate from his grandfather in 1753. Indeed it was principally under 'Great' Daniel's descendants that Islay received its most lasting improvements, though they also managed to dissipate the family fortune. It is unlikely that 'Great' Daniel, the 'hard-faced Merchant oligarch' would have allowed that to happen.

It is generally accepted that one of the main reasons why Islay developed such a concentration of distilling is that following the Act of Union when the Excise Act came into force, for some unknown reason Islay was neglected or exempted from this Act and as a consequence had no Excise officer for 90 years. It is hard not to suspect the hand of 'Great' Daniel in this.

The Shawfield Campbells were improvers and under their rule on Islay the new towns of Bowmore, Port Ellen, Port Charlotte and Port Wemyss were created, as well as the Round Church at Bowmore, but it was 'Great' Daniel Campbell of Shawfield who founded the dynasty and created the wealth that sustained it for many years.

IAIN OG ILE —
THE LAIRD THAT NEVER WAS

No book that draws on the traditional tales of Islay can fail to acknowledge the debt due to John Francis Campbell for his initiative in collecting Gaelic stories in the 19th century. In addition, however, the man is in many ways a legend himself, particularly to the people of Islay.

Born in 1821, John Francis was the son of Walter Frederick Campbell and his first wife Ellenore. Though he was educated at Eton in fine aristocratic tradition, he was also tutored at home, in the setting of the very grand Islay House. More radically, his parents gave him over to the care of a Gaelic speaking piper, also called John Campbell, who introduced him to many of the local folk including story tellers;

from him I learned a good many useful arts. I learned to be hardy and healthy and I learned Gaelic, I learned to swim and take care of myself, and to talk to everybody who chose to talk to me. My kilted nurse and I were always walking about in foul weather or fair, and every man, woman and child had something to say to us. Thus I made acquaintance with a blind fiddler who could recite stories. I worked with the carpenters; I played shinty with all the boys about the farm; and so I got to know a good deal about the ways of Highlanders by growing up as a Highlander myself.

John Francis was only 11 years old, in 1842, when his mother died. This was obviously a great blow for him and his father alike. The lighthouse at Port Ellen was built the same year and carries a moving testimony from Walter Frederick to his wife in the following poem, rich in lighthouse metaphors;

Ye who 'mid storms and tempests stray
In danger's midnight hour,
Behold, where shines this heavenly ray
And hail its guardian power

Tis but faint emblem of her light,
My fond and faithful guide,
Whose sweet example, meekly bright,
Led through this world's eventful tide
My happy course aright.

And still my guiding star she lives
In realms of bliss above,
Still to my heart blest influence gives
And prompts to deeds of love.

'Tis she that bids me on the steep
kindle the beacon's flame,
To light the wanderer o'er the deep,
Who, safe, shall bless her name,

So may sweet virtue lead your way,
That when life's voyage is o'er,
Secure like her, with her you may
Attain the heavenly shore.

The towns of Port Ellen and Port Wemyss were both named after Ellenore Campbell, who was the daughter of the Earl of Wemyss.

Walter Frederick Campbell may have been a poet, a romantic and a determined

143

improver but he was no hard-headed business man or capitalist. It was during his tenure that the island saw its population increase to the highest ever level and the disastrous arrival of the potato famine. Walter Frederick did whatever he could to ease the suffering of his people, including waiving rents. The result was that in 1847 he found himself unable to pay his debts to the bank and lost the island.

The Campbells left in November that year. It is said that John Francis spent some hours kneeling at his mother's grave, which is inside the Bowmore Round Church, before leaving his beloved island home. Walter Frederick went to live in Normandy and his son went off to study law at Edinburgh University.

To the ordinary folk of Islay this was a sad time. The young John Francis (Iain Og Ile to the islanders) was well known and much loved and the community thought wistfully of him as the laird who never was. They looked back at his father's time as a time of improvement and humanity and believed that under the young Campbell things would have continued to be managed in their interests. Instead they got factors, installed by the new owners – faceless, soulless banks, who insisted on the payment of rents. The inevitable outcome was a further wave of clearances and periods of discontent. The island was eventually divided into lots and sold to various new lairds. The days of compassion were over.

Here is a verse from a *Song by an Old Islayman*, found in *The Wiles of the World*, edited by Donald E. Meek. The old Islayman was

Hugh MacCorkindale who emigrated in the 19th century to Sullivan, Ontario; he is clearly lamenting the end of the Campbells' tenure as Lairds of the island.

San Eilean Ileach bha mi og
Duin' nasal còir b'e 'n t-uachdaram,
Bha e math don duine bhochd,
'S cha d'rinn e lochd air tuathanach;
Ach chaill e 'n t-àite, nib ha craiteach,
Rinn seo naisinch fhuadach;
Tha gach taigh is baile fàs
'S tha caoraich 'n àite 'n t-sluaigh ann.

I spent my youth in the Isle of Islay,
And a fair gentleman was the landlord;
He was kind to the pauper,
And did no wrong to farmers;
But he lost the place, a painful matter,
Causing natives to be evicted;
Every house and township is empty
And sheep replace the people.

Nothing is ever simple, but to the islanders it must have seemed that an age of positive improvement and humanity – new towns, new roads, distilleries – and the gentle touch of Walter Frederick Campbell during the famine, was sadly being lost and they were sure that things could have been different under the laird that never was. John Francis became a figure of exaggerated stature to the islanders, not very different from the heroic position that Bonnie Prince Charlie enjoyed in the eyes of the Highlanders a century before.

John Francis qualified in Law and in

1851 was called to the bar in London. The rest of his life was spent either in London, or travelling around the world. Only twice did he return to Islay. He did not practise as a barrister for long, feeling it was not his true calling. His cousin was the eighth Duke of Argyll, and largely as a result of his patronage and connections (he was initially appointed as the Duke's Private Secretary) John Francis inhabited the rarefied air of the inner sanctum of the Royal Court.

He was soon recognised however, as a very able individual and was eventually appointed as secretary to various Royal Commissions, including Heating and Ventilation, Mines, Coal and Lighthouses. These he performed diligently, acquitting himself extremely well.

As can be surmised from the subject matter of those Commissions, he had a particular interest in matters of science and technology and was a founder member of the Photographic Society of London. As early as 1853 he had invented an instrument for measuring sunlight, later known as the Campbell-Stokes heliometer; it continued to be used at Greenwich for almost 150 years. He published a number of books combining his interest in science and travel, for example *Frost and Fire*, a book about glaciers and volcanoes.

In 1874 he was appointed as Groom-in-Waiting in Ordinary to Queen Victoria. He travelled in many countries, throughout Europe and in Russia, Asia and North America, learned to speak at least 10 languages well and had a passing acquaintance with about 15 more.

However, his passion seems to have been Gaelic and Gaeldom and his abiding project was the collection of Gaelic tales. His love of these stories started when he was a boy on Islay and his travels abroad and his life in London made him aware of the value of the Gaelic culture on the one hand and its fragility on the other. John Francis did do some field collecting himself, but mostly the tales were gathered by others under his employment. These included Hector McLean of Ballygrant and John Dewar. The amount of material gathered was huge and much of it remains unpublished; a testimony to the amount of money and time invested in the endeavour by John Francis and his fellow enthusiasts.

The most tangible result of this project is the four volume collection *Popular Tales of the West Highlands*, published in 1862 and *Leabhair na Feinne; Heroic Gaelic Ballads Collected in Scotland Chiefly from 1512 to 1871*, published in 1872. Campbell described himself as a 'storiologist'.

John Francis Campbell's methods of tale gathering are of particular interest here. Many of the informants were reluctant to divulge their stories to collectors because they were inherently suspicious, feared ridicule and also knew that the church frowned on the content of many of these Celtic tales. The good folk of Glencoe refused to offer a single tale when they learned that the senior storiologist was a Campbell. But John Francis had a secret weapon! He is quoted in Aonghas Mac-Kechnie's book *Two Islay monuments and two Islay people*; 'the old chaps are not very willing to say them, the Free Church Ministers are against all these nonsense they say, but by promising them a good reward and a drap of the Crathur I think since they know me that I will be able to get some [tales] from them.'

There is a famous photograph, taken in 1870, of John Francis Campbell and Hector Maclean, both sporting impressive beards, collecting stories from Islayman Lachy MacNeill, in a tenement in Paisley. Sure enough, there is a bottle of whisky on the table, though it appears that Lachy, who looks slightly nervous and deferential, is the only one with a glass; a glass that appears to be empty. Perhaps Lachy is waiting for a fill-up before he gives the next instalment of what was one of the longest and perhaps a rather dry tale to tell — *The Tale of Kane's Leg*.

The tales published by John Francis and his collecting methodology provided a major inspiration to me in working on this book. Though not in any way a collector trying to winkle stories out of informants, I nonetheless found, as any innocent visitor to Islay often does, how much more easily stories flow and indeed become more animated when the cork is drawn from a bottle of the Crathur!

Iain Og Ile died in 1885 at Cannes, where his grave is surmounted by a replica of the Kildalton Cross. Two years later, the people of Islay raised a monument in his memory. That monument stands at Cnoc na Dàl near the head of Loch Indaal, not far from Islay House. The original was practically destroyed by lightning in a storm in 1911 and a replacement had to be re-designed and then erected on the same spot. Very few people have been honoured in this way by the people of Islay; Iain Og Ile, his memory and his legacy have indeed been loved and respected by the islanders.

LEGENDARY FOLK OF LAPHROAIG

My friend and fellow whisky writer Hans Offringa has co-written a book with Marcel van Gils, called *The Legend of Laphroaig*. That book is a biography of a very interesting distillery and a record of some legendary bottles that might make many a collector's mouth water. However, just as it is people who make whisky, it is people who make legends and Laphroaig seems to have more shadows of legendary figures dancing and flickering around it than the other distilleries on Islay.

Donald Johnston – burned in whisky

Laphroaig Distillery was established in 1815 by brothers Donald and Alexander Johnston. Donald was the natural business-man and distiller of the two and eventually bought out his brother in 1836 for £350. Within months Alexander got married to Flora MacTaggart and they went to live in Australia, where he did not make whisky, perhaps missing a trick.

Donald was now sole owner of the dis-tillery but it was about this time that the Laird, Walter Francis Campbell, leased adjoining land to the Stein brothers, James and Andrew, who were part of a dis-tilling dynasty from Clackmannan. They quickly established the Ardenistiel (or Ardenistle) distillery. Donald tried to prevent the building of this distillery, say-ing that the water supply could not sup-port two distilleries. He was unsuccessful but in fact the Ardenistiel distillery had a very unhappy career, eventually being taken over by Donald's son Dugald who closed it down and incorporated much of the buildings and plant into an expansion of Laphroaig.

Donald, who was born in 1796, was married twice. Before that it seems he fathered an illegitimate son James in 1820. He married Isabella MacDougall in 1829 and the couple had five children, the last being also called Isabella (born 1840). Some time after that Isabella died and then he married Alice MacDougall in 1843. Though she had the same surname as the first wife, it is not clear whether they were related. Donald and Alice had one daughter.

In June 1847 the unfortunate Donald is said to have tumbled into a vat of burnt ale (or spent lees) from his own distillery. Did he fall or was he pushed? Whatever happened, the burnt ale was extremely hot and Donald died after two days of horrible agony, destined to become the unfortunate victim who is always referred to by anyone writing a paragraph about this illustrious distillery. The name D. Johnston is still to be seen on bottles of Laphroaig though that actually refers to Dugald Johnston for Donald's son later claimed to have been the founder. In fact Dugald was only 11 years old when his father died and though he inherited the business, as the only legitimate son, it had to be managed on his behalf (by his uncle Walter Graham of Lagavulin) until he was old enough to take over.

Ian Hunter – out-manoeuvred the opposition

Ian Hunter (his family took over from the Johnstons, to whom they were related, in the first few years of the 20th century) inherited the Laphroaig lease in 1919 and finally purchased it from the Ramsays in 1923. However he had been involved in managing the place from about 1908 when he finished his engineering studies in Glasgow. He didn't have to wait long for problems to arise. For decades the Mackie family, who owned Lagavulin, had acted as agents for Laphroaig. In 1908 the contract was not renewed. This annoyed Peter Mackie (known as 'restless' Peter) and he did everything he could to get back at Laphroaig. He built a new distillery in the grounds of Lagavulin, called Malt Mill, to make Laphroaig style whisky and he enticed Laphroaig's distiller to come and work for him. He blocked up the water supply to Laphroaig with stones and he fought Hunter in the courts. Nothing worked – the quietly solid and determined Hunter took everything that the restless, agitated Peter could throw at him and came out on top.

However, the experience is said to have made Hunter very suspicious and secretive and it seems that the thing he valued most in his employees was loyalty and discretion. Hunter's main reputation at Laphroaig was that of improving and expanding the distillery during the 1920s and '30s. He did great things for the distillery and for the brand. One of his triumphs was to be able to continue selling whisky in the United States during prohibition. He convinced people in authority that Laphroaig was a medicinal product. Unwitting officials probably accepted this on the basis that anything that tastes so challenging must be good for you.

In 1928 at the request of the laird of Islay House, who wanted a whisky for his son's coming of age party that would not overpower the refined palate of influential visitors and a mob of aristocratic youngsters, Hunter created a blend based on Laphroaig mixed with Glen Grant, Glenlivet and some grain whiskies. It was christened Islay Mist and proved to be a great success. It is still going strong, and with its emblem of the Great Seal of Islay, is the official whisky of the Royal National Mod, that icon of Scottish Gaeldom.

Ian Hunter died in 1954. He had never married and had no children. It appeared that none of his relatives were interested in becoming involved with Laphroaig so he left the whole place in his will to the distillery manager, Bessie Williamson. And so the distillery passed out of the hands of the Johnston/Hunter family after 140 years.

Bessie Williamson – the whisky matriarch

Elizabeth (Bessie) Leitch Williamson was born in Glasgow in 1908. When she was only eight years old her father was killed in action in the First World War. Her mother raised Bessie and her brother and sister alone. It is quite an achievement that she graduated from Glasgow University in 1932. While waiting for a teaching job to come up, she took a temporary job with her uncle's accountancy firm. Then in 1934, while on holiday on Islay, she applied for a temporary vacancy as a shorthand typist at Laphroaig, intending to stay for three months.

She obviously came to love the island and stayed on, eventually becoming an indispensable aid as personal secretary to Ian Hunter. In 1938 Hunter suffered a stroke while in America and Bessie was sent out to the USA to lend a hand. This was something she was to prove extremely good at and in later years operated as a kind of whisky ambassador on behalf of the Scotch Whisky Association, mainly in North America. Anyway, because of Hunter's failing health she was appointed distillery manager in 1940. Hunter had a reputation for being a difficult customer to deal with and his managers would usually last no more than a few months, but Bessie obviously had what it took and she stayed on in that role until his death in 1954.

When Ian Hunter died his will left Bessie the distillery, Ardenistiel House, the island of Texa and £5,000 in cash. His will conferred £100 on each of the distillery workers who had served for more than 10 years. Rachel McAffer, the secretary was left £1,000 'for saving my life on two occasions.' Inevitably there was gossip and speculation — if Rachel got £1,000 for saving his life twice — what on earth had Bessie done? How was it that this man who was considered to be fond of women, never married and had such a close relationship with his distillery number one, appointing her as manager and leaving the whole place to her in his will? How did she get on so well with him when all the other managers

had found him so difficult? It was even rumoured that he never allowed the young Bessie to have any boyfriends. Whatever the tittle tattle might have been, there was no evidence of anything other than a straight-forward business relationship between them. Perhaps it is as simple as this — the great love of Hunter's life was a well-run Laphroaig and the great love of Bessie's was Islay; after all she came for three months and stayed for her whole life.

There is something legendary about Bessie's reputation. She was often described as the first woman to run or own a distillery. In fact this is not true — the MacDougall sisters, Margaret and Flora, ran Ardbeg in the 1850s, Lucy Ramsey took over Port Ellen in 1892 and Elizabeth Cummings ran and owned Cardhu from 1872 to 1893. The most that can be said is that she was the first woman on Islay in the 20th century to manage and own a distillery. Yet the legend of the distillery matriarch persists. Perhaps it was because she performed such an international role in the 1960s when working with the SWA abroad. She was after all awarded the Woman of the Year in Great Britain in the 1950s and was awarded the Order of St John by the Queen.

She ran Laphroaig successfully, without doubt, though she eventually sold out to Long John Distillers, knowing that without them the distillery could not receive the capital investments and improvements that it needed. However, as the award for charity work suggests, she was a philanthropist by nature and that reflects on her style of running the distillery. The master distiller brought in by Long John was John MacDougall and he describes in his book *Wort, Worms and Washbacks* how she had become a bit of a soft touch, 'Bessie was very much the figurehead of Laphroaig when I went there, and was greatly loved by the staff and the local community. Laphroaig had become known locally as Islay's second Labour Exchange because Bessie could not listen to a hard-luck story without giving in and providing a job for the person concerned, even though there was usually no job at all.' Whatever the gossips and tale-tellers might have to say about her, Bessie was a kind woman and was loved by her staff and by the people of Islay.

NORMAN CAMPBELL

I met Norman Campbell a number of times out on the Glenegadale Moss where he would demonstrate his art of peat cutting to whisky tourists. He always seemed to be the strong silent type, a big, lumbering man, hefting wet peats out of the dark oozing muck and tossing them over his head with ease and panache. He would delight in handing over his awkward, long-handled, queer-spaded peat cutter to visitors who thought it didn't look too difficult and smiling wryly at their pathetic attempts at getting it to budge from the sucking, quivering bog. He was Arthur, drawing the sword from the stone and deftly shoving it back so that hopeful wannabes could embarrass themselves by having a go, getting red in the face from exertion and failure before landing on their arses in the glaur.

One time, while the Lanarkshire Songwriters were vainly struggling to extract fuel from the bog under his desultory tuition, Norman showed me his photograph album. Amazingly, he had photographs of mammoth tusks that he had recovered from the peat hag. I asked what had happened to them and he vaguely answered that some guys from Edinburgh had taken them away for analysis. They had promised to return them but never did.

Norman had various claims to be a whisky legend, not least his unmistakable face, which seemed to appear in so many photographs (see e.g. Charles MacLean's book *Malt Whisky* p. 108). Sadly he died in February 2006 just short of his 60th birthday. Bruichladdich immediately produced a whisky in tribute to Norman. It was the third edition of Bruichladdich 3D — the Peat Proposal. This third edition, called 3D3, was the first whisky ever to have a component of Octomore, the most highly-peated whisky ever made, so it was a fitting tribute to Norrie, the last peat-cutter on Islay. According to the Bruichladdich website,

the recipe for 3D3 was devised with Norrie in mind and reflects his nature — passionate, warm and full of character. According to Jim McEwan, though, one of the reasons for Norman's heroic status on Islay was that 'he once single handedly wiped out the whole Islay Police Department by running his car into the one and only police vehicle on the island as a result of which he was the first person on the island to have a breathalyzer test. The Ileach (local islanders) were so overjoyed that they had a week-long party to celebrate.'

Jim has many other stories involving Norman Campbell, including a hilarious account of the time he had Norman, in a seriously inebriated state, did a virtual peat-cutting workshop and demonstration for journalists in the bar of the George Hotel in Inveraray.

Then there was the time when Norman and his friend James Baker decided to head for the bright lights of London. After a ferry trip spent at the bar, a bottle of whisky on the bus and a carry-out on the London train, they arrived in London in a very sorry state indeed. A London police-man, originally from Glasgow, spied them, quickly confirmed the state they were in and shoved them politely but firmly onto the next train out of the station. They ended up in Coventry and somehow got from there to Inverness. Inverness was still a big city to these boys and this was perhaps the biggest adventure of Norman's life.

Perhaps that is what gave him a taste for fast music and flashing lights, for it was shortly after this that he unleashed his Revolving Disco on the unsuspecting Record Hop club in the Ramsey Hall in Port Ellen. Jim McEwan recalls that usually the only thing revolving was Norman. Norman him-self admitted that, though there was no licensed bar in the hall, whisky was com-monly smuggled past the Council author-ities, concealed in under-garments and was therefore often consumed at slightly higher than room temperature.

Embracing a kind of local show-busi-ness stardom and celebrity status, Norman changed his name to Norrie Kimble, bor-rowing the surname from the character in the 1960s TV show The Fugitive, and ran his Revolving Disco for over 15 years. With his signature Stetson hat, expensive silk shirts, bootlace tie, Country and Western belt buckle and permanently dirty hands, he wowed youngsters across the island with his modern dance records and ultra violet lights (Norman said, 'with those lights it's best to keep your mouth shut if you have false teeth').

As well as the weekend night-time job, Norrie continued to cut peats by hand. This was a hard, demanding, back-breaking job – out in all weathers, buffeted by winds, caught out by rain storms that appeared from no-where and baked (occasionally) by the sun. Add to this, the hangovers, the midges and the diet of whisky and Ambrosia Creamed Rice and you have to admire the strength required to carry it off without complaining, which Norman never did.

He undoubtedly became a legend in his life-time and is now fittingly immortal-ized on a whisky label, reminding us of a time when the peat and Islay whisky were brought together by the sweat of hard-working men.

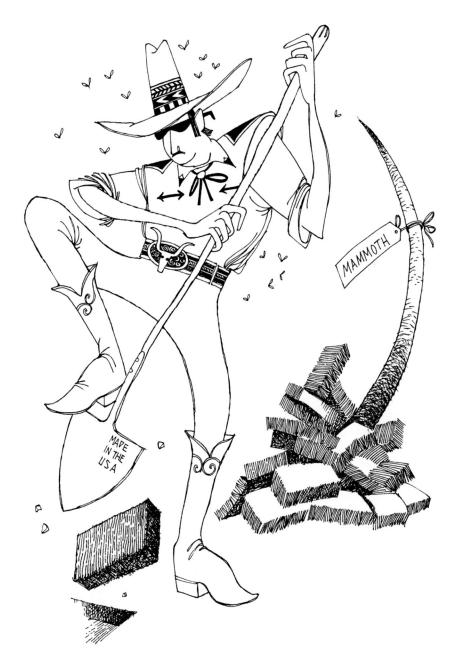

PILLAGER!

The concept of pillaging is not completely unknown in Islay's history; the Lords of the Isles probably brought back booty and pillaged loot from countless raids. Of course they in turn learned it from the Vikings who are supposed to have struck terror in the hearts of west coast Scots when their longships came into view. Recent revisionist archaeological accounts have tried to suggest that the Vikings were actually quite a cultured lot, more interested in male grooming than in pillaging, but the image of Hagar the Horrible is now too deeply ingrained in our collective imagination.

More recently there have been other pillaging incidents. John Paul Jones, the founder of the American Navy (who was born in Kirkcudbright) is supposed to have captured the Islay packet in the Sound of Islay in 1778 (or 1780 – reports vary) and robbed the passengers, including a Major Campbell who was returning from India with his young wife and his entire fortune on his person in the form of gold and jewels. Major Campbell arrived home with nothing left of his fortune; fortunately his land holdings were able to furnish him another eventually. John Paul Jones captured a number of vessels near Islay; The *True Blooded Yankee* did the same in 1813.

What is not normally associated with pillaging is the idea of asking and consent being given. In fact, by definition, the act is then no longer pillaging, but then the modern day 'pillage of malt' masterminded by Kevin Campbell of Lagavulin distillery was always designed as a charitable exercise, so that is probably OK.

You might expect a pillager to be a bit of a hell-raiser but Kevin is more of a fundraiser and has been thinking up various schemes to benefit charities for some time. One of his early efforts, in 2001, involved rolling whisky barrels around Islay. He also organises the Splash for Cash, which involves a group of certifiable friends leaping into the sea off Lagavulin pier on Boxing Day. This mad event has now happened seven times, with the most successful involving over 50 people leaping lemming-like into a cold plunge-pool ocean for little more reward than a hot whisky toddy and the joy of helping to raise £6,000 for charity. Diageo, Kevin's employer, doubles up any funds raised.

Kevin's most successful idea, the Pillage of Malt, first took place in 2003. Kevin and a group of volunteers, mostly other distillery workers, rowed around Islay in Jim MacFarlane's skiff *Kathleen*. The adventure took place on 4 and 5 July, visiting all seven Islay distilleries and exacting 25 litres of 10 year old cask strength malt from each of them. This 'pillaged' malt was then married into a cask at Lagavulin before being bottled some months later as a vatted malt at 57.1% abv. Lagavulin also donated the bottles and boxes and Bruichladdich did the bottling. The 243 bottles were sold in a silent auction with a minimum bid of £100. The result was a fund-raising haul of over £25,000, which was evenly split between the RNLI and Macmillan Cancer Support.

So encouraged were the rowers and

support team that they decided to repeat the stunt in 2005. This time, they were much more ambitious, increasing the booty from 25 litres to 40 litres of 12 year old cask strength malt, and not just from Islay, this was to be a Celtic Pillage Malt, including contributions plundered from Jura and Bushmills distilleries. The extra rowing involved was considerable, but the rewards were great.

The 2005 pillage was carried out using two boats. On a June day in 2005, they started out from Jura in the *Kathleen*, rowing and sailing around Islay, then fairly late on the second day set off for the Antrim coast, a distance of 20 miles. The weather was not particularly nice and the *Kathleen* was replaced by the slightly bigger *James Kelly*, an Irish skiff owned and captained by Robin Ruddock. At times the weather reached gale force 6 and the *James Kelly* had to be taken under tow, once or twice, by one of the support vessels, but the intrepid pillagers were not daunted. It would take more than a bit of weather to keep these modern day Vikings from getting their hands on the Bushmills loot. Interestingly, the boat was a fishing yawl, of a type sometimes known as a Drontheim, named after the Norwegian town. These boats, still used from the Great Lakes to Japan, and especially in Northern Ireland, are direct descendents of the Viking longboat.

The spoils of that pillage amounted to a prize of 500 bottles of 12 year old whisky at 55.8% abv; these were bottled at Bruichladdich distillery (who also donated the bottles and boxes) in February 2006.

After some skilful publicity (Michael Palin was brought 'on board' to help the cause) the silent internet auction raised the sum of £42,000, this time shared mainly between the Children's Hospice Associations of Scotland and of Northern Ireland. These bottles were given a peculiarly lopsided label, designed (all labels have been designed by Clive Bruce) presumably to give the impression they were slapped on while the boat was rocking or while the pillagers were either fleeing with their purloined proceeds or else, having escaped, staggering drunk from their success.

The 2007 pillage took place at the end of June (the trip, scheduled for 30 June, was brought forward a day because of a bad weather forecast). The boat used in 2007 was another Irish built vessel – a skerries yawl called the *Isis*. The *Isis* was purchased and donated to the pillagers by Iain Smith, a retired policeman living on Islay. That boat is now a community-owned asset and part of the proceeds of the 2007 pillage were kept back for the upkeep of the vessel.

This third pillage gathered the equivalent of 250 bottles from the Islay and Jura distilleries and this time the money raised was largely allocated according to the wishes of these distilleries, each one dispensing £2,500 to charities that they themselves nominated. Concurrent with the boat voyage, some other volunteers took part in a 56 mile barrel rolling trek around Islay. The idea was for the barrel rollers to race the pillagers. In fact they all ended up at Jura distillery with only seven minutes between them, so the result was considered a draw.

The barrel rollers possibly had the hardest job though, as jogging along the road rolling a whisky barrel is not easy. They were no doubt inspired by the thought of sampling all the collected whiskies and the final blend after their exertions. I have offered a few drams to participants myself, but not one of them will divulge who was inside the barrel.

It has been said that 2007 was to be the final pillage but Kevin told me that he is secretly planning a grand finale, which might happen in three or four years and might take the form of a Classic Pillage, shadowing the Classic Malts cruise and so gathering malt from Talisker, Oban and Lagavulin. That would involve quite a few sea miles and the planning would be even more of a challenge.

These Pillaged Malts are very rare and are set to become collectors' items, especially if one is lucky enough to acquire the whole set. Some bottles are already selling for £450 or more. A local charity, Islay Disabled Endeavours and Action (IDEAS), ironically had their bottle of pillaged malt stolen in a burglary. Kevin was able to acquire a replacement and the charity now has a full set.

Is the whisky any good? After all it is hardly the way any serious blender would approach the task of creating a great whisky. I was in the Bruichladdich bottling hall in February 2006 when the second pillage was bottled and had a chance to try it and in my opinion it was a very agreeable dram indeed. I have also tasted the 14 year old (2007) pillage and was utterly amazed at how gorgeous this dark, smoky complex malt tasted; if you want to acquire one of the pillages to drink that would be my recommendation.

Kevin Campbell is becoming a bit of a legend on Islay for his imaginative and successful fundraising ideas. The time and commitment, the effort and care needed to plan and carry out these events is not to be under-estimated. He, and of course his colleagues and volunteers are to be praised for their efforts. What makes the events such a success is that the participants are involved in an adventure and have a lot of fun in the process. So what will he come up with next in the context of Viking misbehaving; pitched battles, drinking contests, kidnappings, the blood eagle? We watch with bated breath.

SEAMUS MOR

Once upon a time on Islay there was a great distillery called Bruichladdich. The distillery manager and his wife were very happy but they had one unfulfilled ambition. They were desperate to have a child. They prayed every night and tried all sorts of herbal concoctions but nothing worked.

Then one day they heard about the effect that Islay cheese was having on the birth rate in Italy and they had a brilliant idea. It happened that Islay cheese was made right next door to the distillery so they both started eating Islay cheese every day. Sure enough within a few weeks the wife fell pregnant and their joy knew no bounds. When their little daughter was born they threw an enormous party. Everyone was invited and of course they all came because they knew there would be plenty of free whisky.

Actually not everyone was invited. One old *cailleach* was left off the list because no one had seen her for a long time. She'd been on Jura for a long visit with her friend from the Paps. When word of this fantastic party spread to Jura the old hag appeared, furious because she had not been invited.

She cast a spell over the whole place and the next morning when the people in the village woke up they could remember nothing and found that the distillery was officially mothballed. The gates were locked and the windows boarded up. Within months a tangle of vicious brambles grew up and the community became depressed. She even put a spell on the cheese factory and it closed down too.

The distillery manager and his family and all the staff had been locked away inside in a twilight limbo of suspended animation, and the spell could only be broken when a great hero would come and free the giant rusty padlock from the gates. Over the years many would-be saviours came to try their strength or cunning. They tried brute force, they tried skeleton keys, and they tried to magic the lock off the iron bars with incantations and passwords. Nothing worked.

One day a syndicate of wise men decided that they would search for the greatest whisky hero in the land and put him onto the job. After many months of searching they discovered that the hero they were seeking was just across the loch in Bowmore all the time.

So it was that they brought Seamus Mor to the gates of Bruichladdich. He stood before the entrance; birds stopped singing, sunbeams glinted through dark clouds upon him and a rainbow appeared across the loch. He took the padlock in his hands and it seemed to crumble to dust. The brambles wilted under his gaze. The gates creaked open and people heard the great distillery slowly cranking into life again after its long sleep.

The old hands at the distillery were dazed and amazed as Seamus put them back to work. The distillery manager and his wife rubbed their eyes. Seamus lifted their baby daughter, kissed her with the practised skill of a politician, and promised her a job in the new bottling plant when she was old enough. The community could not believe their good fortune and celebrated with a drunken spree that some say went on a bit too long. The old *cailleach* fled back to Jura and was never seen on Islay again.

Seamus went on to become an even greater hero, not just locally but through-out the whole whisky world. No doubt he lived happily ever after too. The only sad thing is that he couldn't do anything for Islay cheese, but then maybe they need to find their own hero.

NOTE: Any perceived similarity between Seamus Mor and Jim McEwan is entirely intentional.

THE LADY AT THE BRIDGEND BAR

This legend has my own clumsy hand in its development. This is how it came about — I was in conversation with a retired blender of my acquaintance (who shall remain nameless) and he was telling me about a time when he was travelling with a group of people (including a well-known broadcaster, who shall also remain nameless) from Jura to the airport at Glenegedale. The weather turned really bad while they were *en route* and heavy snow started to fall. They could proceed no further than the Bridgend Hotel and had to take refuge from the storm in there.

They were well looked after but could not leave for many hours. Drams were taken and conversation roamed far and wide. At one point the name of a certain whisky writer (whom I shall not name) came up and my friend made a comment, which he slowly realised from various glances and body language clues, was a bit of a *faux pas*. He told me that he suddenly realised that the whisky writer in question must have been 'having a fling with the lady from the Bridgend Bar.'

There was something in that line that made me think it belonged in a song. I did nothing about it myself, but must have mentioned the line to a couple of people who worked their own magic with it. The poem, by my mother-in-law, Edith Ryan and the song by my friend Billy Stewart are given below.

I also mentioned this to Henry Munro, husband of fellow musician Norma Munro, and he told me that there was once a barmaid at the Bridgend Bar who, notoriously, used to sunbathe in the garden next to the hotel with no clothes on. She was obscured from the road by a wall, invisible to all, except drivers of vans, lorries and higher vehicles. Apparently there were a few near misses due to drivers not keeping their eyes on the road. This is not a corroborated story and there is no suggestion that the two women were the same.

O'GRADY'S LADY - A RONDEL

He was having a fling with a lady
Who worked in the Bridgend Bar.
He told her his name was O'Grady:
Said he'd worshiped her from afar,
And he told us nothing was shady —
That her door was always ajar.
He was having a fling with a lady
Who worked in the Bridgend Bar.

He thought she was in her hay day
And no words we said would mar
The way he felt about Sadie
For, wasn't she well above par.
He was having a fling with a lady
And she worked in the Bridgend Bar.

Edith Ryan

THE BARMAID FAE THE BRIDGEND BAR

There's a wummin tends a bar and men come
from near and far
To Islay just to catch a glimpse they try
But if she turns roon fast what they see could
be their last
For she's big enough tae poke oot baith yer eyes

CHORUS

She's the barmaid fae the Bridgend Bar
She's the Barmaid fae the Bridgend Bar
Her figure is exciting like a bag o rabbits fighting
She's the Barmaid fae the Bridgend Bar

When she pulls a pint Oh man it's such a sight
It's enough to stop the heart of any male
With what's sticking oot in front she can
hardly see the pumps
Aye the whole thing is accomplished using
Braille

When the sun begins tae shine she like to take
some time
Tae sunbathe au naturale oot on the grass
And Bridgend is alive as the locals they are
driving
Aroon tae catch a glimpse as she goes past

CHORUS

She's the barmaid fae the Bridgend Bar
She's the Barmaid fae the Bridgend Bar
Her figure is exciting like a bag o rabbits fighting
She's the Barmaid fae the Bridgend Bar

She walks with a wiggle and other bits that
jiggle
She has bother keeping bits where they belong
And she causes quite a fuss when she's running
for a bus
Man I didnae know cahootchie was that strong

She is the stuff of legends and there is no point
in hedging
It appears that she was quite free with her
charms
But if you take advantage then I think there's
every chance
That you'll no longer be rolling in your sweet
babies arms

Words and Music: Billy Stewart (Garriongill
Music)

THE LADY OF THE ISLES

A small minibus zips around Islay, emblazoned with the logo 'Lady of the Isles'. The Lady is Christine Logan, another legendary Ileach with the typical warmth and enthusiasm often found in the people of Islay. Christine worked at Bowmore Distillery for 25 years, being awarded Distillery Visitor Centre Manager of the Year in 2003 by Whisky Magazine. Then she left Bowmore to set up on her own as an Islay tour guide providing customised services for visitors to the island. In 2006 she received the Whisky Ambassador of the year award.

Christine's parents had some legendary status also. Her mother, Lily 'the fish' MacDougall, is an outstanding character and her father, Dougie MacDougall, was the Lighthouse Boatman at Port Askaig for 45 years and wrote two books of stories about Islay life, *As Long as Water Flows* and *Still Waters Run Deep*.

One of my earliest memories of Christine was when I visited Bowmore distillery with my wife in 1996. Christine told us about the Swimming Pool next door, which was heated by waste water from the distillery. 'Have you been in to the swimming pool?' she asked. Unfortunately we hadn't, we replied, because my wife had forgotten to bring a swimming costume. 'Hold on just a minute,' she said and, opening a filing cabinet drawer, she produced a lady's swimming costume. We didn't ask how it came to be there, just borrowed it – it was a bit on the baggy side but it allowed us to enjoy the delights of the MacTaggart Pool, including the sauna which, as an antidote to cold weather on Islay, comes close second to a large dram. Such was the resourcefulness of Christine Logan.

Christine is of course a repository of stories about Islay and she likes nothing better than to talk to her clients as she drives them around the hot spots of the island. Many of her clients are from Japan, where she has a huge reputation, celebrity status and a dedicated website. Christine has appeared on television in Japan and one of the stories I heard about her concerns something that happened at one of the Whisky Live events in Tokyo.

She had agreed to be involved in a practical joke set up by some of the Distillery Managers (no names) to catch out Iain Henderson of Laphroaig. Iain was on the stage, in front of a large audience, to receive an award. Along came the bearer of the award – a Japanese Geisha in full costume, from the clip-clopping platform shoes and the kimono to the chopstick hair combs, white face and red lips. Only when the Geisha spoke did Iain realise it was Christine – he nearly fainted.

Another story, which Christine herself told me, concerns a bottle of whisky that she counts as one of her prize possessions, and which she refers to as Paul's Dram. This came from a cask of Bowmore whisky that was filled in 1965 for Paul Stewart, son of racing driver, Jackie Stewart. Tim Morrison of Morrison-Bowmore was the boy's godfather and Rob Roy whisky sponsored Jackie Stewart's car at that time. The cask was finally bottled as a 41 year old and Christine has one of the few bottles, with its unusual label designed by artist Craigie Aitchison.

Apparently, four or five years before it was bottled, Christine received a call from the *Hebridean Princess* asking if some of their cruise passengers could have a distillery tour. It turned out it was a rather special party, including Jackie Stewart, his wife, their son Paul and Sir Sean Connery. Apart from the fact that Christine was excited and emotional at seeing Paul, the 36 year old owner of the 36 year old cask, she treated the group as any other, showing them round 'her' distillery with pride. Some drams were sampled and the group prepared to depart. Jackie Stewart had been warm and affable throughout and gave Christine two kisses as

thank you and farewell. Sean Connery had been more aloof throughout and sat quietly on the bus front seat. Christine stood at the front, the mother hen waving goodbye to her chickens. Refusing to let Mr Connery slide out of the lime-light, she planted a large kiss on his bald head and pirouetted down the bus steps.

That is typical of Christine – larger than life, indomitable, full of fun. Now she is no longer an ambassador for only for Bowmore but for the whole of Islay, it will be interesting to see what other stories will arise.

THE PRINCE HAS LANDED
(A DIFFERENT KIND OF CHARLIE)

Prince Charles, Prince of Wales, Duke of Cornwall, Duke of Rothesey and Lord of the Isles, visited Islay on 29 June 1994. In the old days, when the main highway was the sea, the Lords of the Isles travelled in their galleys, which, given conditions of tide and weather, might require enormous skill in sailing. Now, all that has changed and it is perhaps appropriate, that the present Lord of the Isles should arrive in a sailing ship of the skies. The Prince was at the helm and although the weather was fine, either his skills or the runway were a bit short. The plane, a BAe 146, landed heavily and with burst tyres, veered off the runway, suffering considerable damage. No one on board was injured in any way. The Prince said to the airport rescue services 'I am afraid I made a right mess of that one.'

The *Ileach* newspaper, in the days following the incident, pointed out that the Prince's plane, by some strange coincidence, landed with its nose pointing directly to a spot on the nearby road where his relative, Prince Christopher of Yugoslavia, had been killed in a tragic road accident, while cycling, just the previous month.

The Prince seemed to keep his composure through the whole incident. His first official visit was to Laphroaig distillery, where he was welcomed by the Islay Pipe Band, representatives of Allied Distillers, and Iain Henderson, distillery manager (a legend in his own right) who gave him a dram. The press were already after the Prince like a pack of wolves because of his televised confession of having had an affair with Camilla; pranging an air-force jet on his way to a distillery was not going to help matters. Despite his impressive air of coolness, if ever a man needed a dram it was probably Charlie at that moment.

Prince Charles is already on record as saying that Laphroaig is his favourite dram, and the distillery had already received the Royal Warrant at the beginning of that year. Fortified by perhaps the most welcome dram of his life, the Prince was able to carry on with the rest of his visit to the island. By the time he was being photographed with the children at Islay High School later in the day, he was looking extremely relaxed indeed.

The damaged jet stayed in position for a number of weeks, becoming a bit of a celebrated tourist attraction and source of amusement for the locals. The authorities quickly erected a tent over the nose of the jet and almost as quickly, locals or anonymous airport personnel, applied tasteful artwork to the tent, which now became 'The Drop Inn' guest house with painted-on curtains and flowers at the window and a pussy cat and a pint of milk at the doorstep.

A team of RAF engineers eventually got the undercarriage sufficiently repaired for the plane to be flown to RAF Benson, where the full repair job was carried out by British

Aerospace engineers. The outcome of the internal enquiry into the cause of the accident is not known and the total cost of the incident has not been made public.

In 2008, the Prince returned to Islay and to Laphroaig Distillery. This time, he was with his wife Camilla, Duchess of Rothesay, and this time they arrived by helicopter from Rothesay; the Prince was not at the controls. Once more the welcome party involved the Black Bottle Islay Pipe Band and children from the Port Ellen primary school. The children and the royal visitors were equally well behaved and the Prince, after trying his hand at turning the malt on the malting floor, continued on his way, he and Camilla both clutching a bottle of Laphroaig whisky.

The Queen's distillery visit

The only time Her Majesty Queen Elizabeth II has visited a distillery was also on Islay. This was in August 1980, when the Queen and her family arrived on the Royal Yacht Britannia; included in the itinerary was a visit to Bowmore distillery. Her Majesty's arrival in Islay was very keenly anticipated by the islanders and the whole island was freshly painted and shining in the summer sun.

The distillery also had a thorough makeover for the visit. Indeed the installation of wooden walkways around the distillery date from this time, though there are divided opinions about whether this was done for the royal visit.

One story that survives from that time concerns the Rolls Royce belonging to the Chairman of Morrison Bowmore, James

Howat. Mr Howat decided that his Rolls Royce should be brought to Islay in order that the Queen might have a hurl in a decent motor. The car was put into the Rolls Royce dealership in Glasgow for a complete service and valet. Driving the spruced up car to the Islay ferry, Mr Howat was involved in an accident with a motorbike on the road along Loch Lomondside. The car suffered significant damage.

Howat phoned the garage in Glasgow, who immediately flew some engineers to Islay. He continued on with the car to the ferry and the team of engineers worked on the car overnight at the distillery. The vehicle was ready in the nick of time and the Queen never knew anything about the frantic efforts taken to provide her with a suitable carriage to carry her around Islay. Bowmore, sadly did not gain a Royal Warrant, but of course Rolls Royce did.

English whisky

It is a well-known fact (one that all primary school children in Scotland are taught) that the reason why the English tried to conquer Scotland for centuries, was in order to learn the secrets of distilling whisky. The poor, hapless English only ever managed to brew beer, while the second part of the process always eluded even their keenest scientists. It is sadly true, that while whisky can turn a country's fighting men into heroes, beer only makes flatulent sluggards; thus the lack of decent spirits had always been considered a matter of national security in England.

There is a rumour that a deal was struck

between Iain Henderson and Prince Charles; in return for the Royal Warrant and some very high profile product endorsement, Iain was persuaded to share the secrets of distillation with the English. The deal was made quietly, when the Prince visited Laphroaig, and though it took a couple of years to set up the first English distillery (Saint George's distillery in Roudham in Norfolk) and though Iain was no longer working at Laphroaig by that time, being a man of his word, Iain kept his promise.

So he went to Roudham where he spent several months trying to teach the English how to make whisky (they had to import the equipment from Scotland too). His contract finished after one year and it is too early to say whether he taught them to make good whisky, as it is not yet mature enough to be judged. However, the whole situation turned out sadly for Iain; he now sits, a broken man, in a small caravan on the English side of the border, hoping that one day the Scots will forgive him and let him return home. There is no sign of that yet — indeed it would take a Conservative victory in the Scottish Parliament, so he might be there for a while. Furthermore, his promised knighthood has not materialised either — perhaps the authorities are waiting to see if his whisky is any good first.

AN ISLAY MALT

Poem By Janette Hannah

I hold within my hand
The Isle
Within the glass.
The life and times
Of loved ones.
The morning dew.
The sea.
The sun.
The sand—
And then, through that,

The smoke from Donald's fire
Comes drifting through the years.
The trout that Susan's man caught.
The breath of deer, then back
To days unsure,
When Somerled did rule
The wild peat covered land.
All this within
The glass within
The hand.

BIBLIOGRAPHY

Black, Ronald (ed), *The Gaelic Underworld* (Birlinn)

Booth, C. Gordon, *An Islay Notebook* (Islay Museums Trust)

Campbell, John Francis, *Popular Tales of the West Highlands* (Edmonston and Douglas)

Campbell, John Francis, *Leabhair na Feinne; Heroic Gaelic Ballads Collected in Scotland Chiefly from 1512 to 1871*

Cribb, Stephen & Julie, *Whisky on the Rocks – origins of the 'water of life'* (British Geological Survey)

Earl, Peggy, *Tales of Islay: Fact and Folklore* (The Celtic House)

van Gils, Marcel & Offringa, Hans, *The Legend of Laphroaig* (Still Publishing)

Hellsing, Lennart, *Cladville Cakes* (MIST)

Hill, Joanna & Bastin, Nicholas, *A Very Canny Scot* (Two Plus George Ltd)

Jefford, Andrew, *Peat Smoke and Spirit* (pub. Headline)

MacDougall, Dougie, *Still Waters Run Deep*

McDougall, John, & Smith, Gavin D., *Wort, Worms & Washbacks* (Neil Wilson Publishing Ltd)

MacKechnie, Aonghas, *Two Islay Monuments and Two Islay People* (Ileach Ltd)

MacNeil, Joe Neil, *Tales Until Dawn*

Martin Martin, *A Description of the Western Islands of Scotland circa 1695* (Birlinn)

Meek, Donald E., *Caran An-t-saoghail (The Wiles of the World)* (Birlinn)

Mitchell, Joseph, *Reminiscences of my life in the Highlands* (David & Charles)

Moir P., & Crawford I., *Argyll Shipwrecks*

Newton, Norman, *Islay* (The Pevensey Press)

Pattison, Thomas, *Gaelic Bards* (A. Sinclair)

Pennant, Thomas, *A Tour in Scotland and Voyage to the Hebrides 1772* (Birlinn)

Philip, Neil, *The Penguin Book of Scottish Folktales* (Penguin Books)

Macdonald Robertson, R., *Selected Highland Folk Tales* (David & Charles)

Seanchas Ìle (Argyll Publishing)

Swire, Otta F., *The Inner Hebrides And Their Legends* (Collins)

Thompson, F. et al, *Lamplighter and Story-Teller: John Francis Campbell of Islay 1821–1885* (National Library of Scotland)

Townsend, Brian, *Scotch Missed* (Neil Wilson Publishing)

Wiggins, J., *The Exmouth of Newcastle 1811 – 1847* (Ileach Teleservices Ltd)

Wilson, Neil, *Scotch and Water* (Lochar Publishing)

Some CDs by ROBIN LAING

One for the Road
(Greentrax 313)

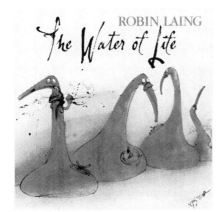

The Water of Life
(Greentrax 246)

The Angels' Share
(Greentrax 137)

Robin Laing has few superiors.
He is heard at his compelling best in
'The Angels' Share'.

THE SCOTSMAN

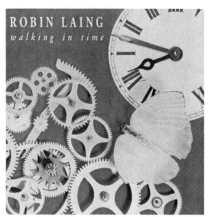

Walking in Time
(Greentrax 072)

Superior craftsmanship...
A very impressive album

THE SCOTSMAN

Edinburgh Skyline
(Greentrax 021)

Demonstrates clearly that he is a
major songwriting talent

EVENING NEWS

Imaginary Lines
(Greentrax 185)

Another first-rate collection by a
master of the genre

THE SCOTS MAGAZINE

Some other books published by **LUATH** PRESS

The Whisky River: Distilleries of Speyside

Robin Laing

ISBN 1 905222 97 1   PBK   £12.99

Which river has half the distilleries in Scotland found along its length and in its surrounding glens?

Were monks at the forefront of developing whisky?

Which Speyside distillery produced chilli-flavoured whisky?

How did Glenrothes distillery expel its ghost?

Robin Laing set out to visit every distillery in the Speyside area, from Benromach to Tomintoul. There are descriptions of over 50 distilleries on Speyside, including The Macallan, The Glenlivet, Cardhu, Aberlour, Glenfiddich and Glengrant.

Each entry is part history, part travelogue and part commentary on the changes in the whisky industry.

Includes personal musings by the author, stories associated with the distillery and snippets of poetry and song.

Laing's 'spirit' guide in his journey is Alfred Barnard, author of 1887s *The Whisky Distilleries of the United Kingdom*. Barnard visited many of the same distilleries that Laing visits now and similarly left his impressions of the state of the facilities and the beauty of the surroundings. Much of this present book compares what Barnard found with what exists now, and the differences – and similarities – are often fascinating.

The Whisky Muse: Scotch whisky in poem & song

Robin Laing

ISBN 1 906307 44 X   PBK   £9.99

Whisky – the water of life, perhaps Scotland's best known contribution to humanity

Muse – goddess of creative endeavour. The Whisky Muse – the spark of inspiration to many of Scotland's great poets and songwriters.

This book is a collection of the best poems and songs, both old and new, on the subject of that great Scottish love, whisky.

I first met Robin Laing and Bob Dewar within the hallowed halls of the Scotch Malt Whisky Society in Leith, where Robin and I sit on the Nosing Panel which selects casks of malt whisky for bottling, while Bob executes the famous cartoons which illustrate our findings and embellish the Society's Newsletter. The panel's onerous job is made lighter by Robin's ability not only to sniff out elusive scents, but to describe them wittily and accurately, and in this unique collection of ninety-five songs and poems about Scotch whisky he has exercised precisely the same skill of sniffing out treasures. As a highly accomplished singer-songwriter, he also describes them authoritatively, while Bob's illustrations add wit and humour. This splendid book is necessary reading for anyone interested in whisky and song. It encapsulates Scottish folk culture and the very spirit of Scotland.

Charles MacLean, Editor at Large, WHISKY MAGAZINE

Riddoch on the Outer Hebrides

Lesley Riddoch
ISBN 1 906307 86 5   PBK   £12.99

Riddoch on the Outer Hebrides is a thought-provoking commentary based on broadcaster Lesley Riddoch's cycle journey through a beautiful island chain facing seismic cultural and economic change. Her experience is described in a typically affectionate but hard-hitting style; with humour, anecdote and a growing sympathy for islanders tired of living at the margins but wary of closer contact with mainland Scotland.

Let's be proud of standing on the outer edge of a crazy mainstream world – when the centre collapses, the periphery becomes central.
ALASTAIR MCINTOSH

She has a way of shining the magnifying glass on a well-documented place in a new and exciting way matching every beauty with a cultural wart that builds to create one of the most unfalteringly real images of the islands – all the more astounding for coming from an outsider.
STORNOWAY GAZETTE

Rum: Nature's Island

Magnus Magnusson
ISBN 0 946487 32 4   PBK   £7.95

Rum: Nature's Island is the fascinating story of a Hebridean island from the earliest times through to the Clearances. It recalls the island in the days it was the sporting playground of a Lancashire industrial magnate, and celebrates its rebirth as a National Nature Reserve, a model for the active ecological management of Scotland's wild places.

Thoroughly researched and written in a lively accessible style, the book includes comprehensive coverage of the island's geology, animals and plants, and people, with a special chapter on the Edwardian extravaganza of Kinloch Castle. There is practical information for visitors to what was once known as the Forbidden Isle; the book provides details of bothy and other accommodation, walks and nature trails. It closes with a positive vision for the island's future: biologically diverse, economically dynamic and ecologically sustainable.

Luath Storyteller: Tales of Whisky
Stuart McHardy
ISBN 1 906817 41 3 PBK £5.99

The truth is of course that whisky was invented for a single, practical reason – to offset Scotland's weather.

Raise your glasses and toast this collection of delightful tales, all inspired by Scotland's finest achievement: whisky. We see how the amber nectar can help get rid of a pesky giant, why you should never build a house without offering the foundations a dram and how it can bring a man back from the brink of death.

Whisky has a long and colourful history in Scotland, causing riots and easing feuds, and McHardy has gathered together stories which have been passed down through many generations, often over a wee nip. *Tales of Whisky* is a tribute to the Scottish sense of humour and love of fine story-telling.

Luath Guides: Mull & Iona – Highways and Byways
Peter McNab
ISBN 1 842820 89 3 PBK £5.99

Peter MacNab takes the visitor on a tour of these two accessible islands of the Inner Hebrides, considered to be the centre of Celtic Christianity. Born and brought up in Mull, the author has an unparalleled knowledge of the island and throughout this book he shows the reader the true Mull and Iona.

Both Mull and Iona are now easily accessible even for day visitors from the mainland, and no parts of Scotland will give more joy to the traveller. Iona, made famous by Columba, founder of Celtic Christianity, represents a spiritual experience rare enough in the world today. The colourful front of Tobermory will welcome you to Mull, an island with fascinating geology to discover amongst the beautiful surroundings of Ben More and Fingal's Cave.

Lewis & Harris: History & Pre-History

Francis Thompson
ISBN 0 946487 77 4 PBK £4.99

The fierce Norsemen, intrepid missionaries and mighty Scottish clans – all have left a visible mark on the landscape of Lewis and Harris. This comprehensive guide explores sites of interest in the Western Isles, from pre-history through to the present day.

Harsh conditions failed to deter invaders from besieging these islands or intrepid travellers from settling, and their legacy has stood the test of time in an array of captivating archaeological remains from the stunningly preserved Carloway Broch, to a number of haunting standing stones, tombs and cairns. With captivating tales – including an intriguing murder mystery and a romantic encounter resulting in dramatic repercussions for warring clans – Francis Thompson introduces us to his homeland and gives us an insight into its forgotten ways of life.

The Islands that Roofed the World: Easdale, Seil etc

Mary Withall
ISBN 0 946487 76 6 PBK £4.99

Come over the 200-year-old bridge which crosses the Atlantic to the charming, yet scarred, Inner Hebridean Slate Islands.

The Slate Islands lie off the west coast of Argyll. Slate has been taken from their shores from earliest recorded history and the richness and quality of the deposits meant that in the 18th and 19th centuries slate quarrying was one of the most important industries in Scotland.

The Breadalbane family owned the land of Easdale and its surrounds for over 400 years and of course roofed their own buildings in slate as well as many important buildings, including Cawdor Castle in Invernesshire and Glasgow Cathedral. Their 18th century ownership of Nova Scotia ensured international trade, and it is therefore unsurprising to find public buildings in eastern Canada roofed in Easdale slate.

The geology, the industry, the people and their way of life: this is the story of the Slate Islands past, present and future, told by the Easdale Folk Museum archivist, with affection and admiration. Easdale remains unique, an island that has no roads and cannot support heavy vehicular traffic. The islanders today are working to retain its delicate environmental and economic balance in a way that is feasible in the modern world.

The Ultimate Burns Supper Book

Clark McGinn
ISBN 1 906817 50 2 PBK £7.99

Everything you need to enjoy or arrange a Burns Supper – just add food, drink and friends.

Clark McGinn, one of the foremost Burns Supper speakers in the world, presents *The Ultimate Burns Supper Book*. Containing all the information you need to enjoy a Supper, whether as host, speaker or guest, this book is full of advice, anecdotes, poetry and wit.

Includes:

- A complete run through of what to expect on the night, with a list of courses and speeches
- Advice on what to wear
- A section on how to prepare and present speeches
- A list of common Burns Supper questions (and their answers!)
- A selection of Burns's greatest poems, including a full English verse translation of the 'Address to a Haggis'
- Answers your concerns about eating haggis and extols the pleasures of drinking whisky

Edinburgh & Leith Pub Guide

Stuart McHardy
ISBN 1 906307 80 6 PBK £5.99

The essential guide to the best pubs in Edinburgh and Leith.

Long familiar with Edinburgh and Leith's drinking dens, watering holes, shebeens and dens of iniquity, Stuart McHardy has penned a bible for the booze connoisseur.

Over 170 pubs
12 pub trails plus maps
New section on clubs
Brief guide to Scottish beers and whiskies
Some notes on etiquette

Whether you're here for Hogmanay, a Six Nations weekend, the Festival, just one evening or the rest of your life, this is the companion to slip in your pocket as you venture out in search of the craic.

Details of these and other books published by Luath Press can be found at: **www.luath.co.uk**

Luath Press Limited

committed to publishing well written books worth reading

LUATH PRESS takes its name from Robert Burns, whose little collie Luath (*Gael.*, swift or nimble) tripped up Jean Armour at a wedding and gave him the chance to speak to the woman who was to be his wife and the abiding love of his life. Burns called one of 'The Twa Dogs' Luath after Cuchullin's hunting dog in Ossian's *Fingal*. Luath Press was established in 1981 in the heart of Burns country, and is now based a few steps up the road from Burns' first lodgings on Edinburgh's Royal Mile.

Luath offers you distinctive writing with a hint of unexpected pleasures.

Most bookshops in the UK, the US, Canada, Australia, New Zealand and parts of Europe either carry our books in stock or can order them for you. To order direct from us, please send a £sterling cheque, postal order, international money order or your credit card details (number, address of cardholder and expiry date) to us at the address below. Please add post and packing as follows: UK – £1.00 per delivery address; overseas surface mail – £2.50 per delivery address; overseas airmail – £3.50 for the first book to each delivery address, plus £1.00 for each additional book by airmail to the same address. If your order is a gift, we will happily enclose your card or message at no extra charge.

Luath Press Limited
543/2 Castlehill
The Royal Mile
Edinburgh EH1 2ND
Scotland
Telephone: 0131 225 4326 (24 hours)
Fax: 0131 225 4324
email: sales@luath.co.uk
Website: www.luath.co.uk